SALES NEGOTIATION STRATEGIES

SALES NEGOTIATION STRATEGIES

MACK HANAN

JAMES CRIBBIN

HOWARD BERRIAN

amacom

A DIVISION OF AMERICAN MANAGEMENT ASSOCIATIONS

Library of Congress Cataloging in Publication Data

Hanan, Mack.
  Sales negotiation strategies.

  Includes index.
    1. Selling. 2. Negotiation. I. Cribbin, James J.,
  joint author. II. Berrian, Howard, joint author.
  III. Title.
  HF5438.25.H35   658.85   76-44021
  ISBN 0-8144-5431-3

© 1977 AMACOM

A division of American Management Associations, New York.

First Printing

To Herman Heiser,

who brought to
our negotiations
a rare mix
of unassailable honesty
with our clients

and a warm,
humane understanding
of us,
his fellows.

Gresham D Hutchings Jr

Foreword

Over the past few years the definition of what it means to have a customer "sold" has radically changed. Back in the days when most selling was done by high-pressure salesmanship, it used to mean having the customer *persuaded*. From the salesman's point of view, this was often an "I win—you lose" approach. The salesman and his customer were adversaries, selling was war, and either the salesman overcame the customer's objections and won the sale or he lost. There was no middle ground, no strong sense of interrelationship, and few mutual goals.

As customer defenses against being persuaded began to catch up with the offense, many salesmen changed to competitive selling. Here the customer is positioned as a competitor, not an adversary. In order to have him sold, the salesman must make him *disadvantaged*. This is an "I give up a little—you give up a little more" approach. Sometimes the customer gets a bad deal or the salesman makes a profitless sale. Both can come away with a deficit instead of a benefit. When this happens, the selling process has mutually disadvantaged them.

Even in today's sophisticated selling environment, where salesmen and their customers are equally adept and both operate at a high level of proficiency in the ploys and counterploys of persuading and disadvantaging each other, selling by these two methods still works. But it is working less well than a third approach that sells a customer by making him *partnered*.

Partnering is an "I win—you win" sales strategy. The process by which it works is called negotiation and its objective can be summarized in this way: to create premium-value/premium-price sales transactions in which the customer receives the premium values of the salesman's benefits and the salesman receives a premium price in return for them. In this way they profit mutually.

Negotiation is the art of making mutually profitable sales agreements. It is not an art of deceptive conversation, manipulative conniving, or erudite flimflamming. The objective of negotiation is to convert a salesman and his customer into partners. For this reason, all the strategies we recommend are designed to create, maintain, and restore partnerships.

We advocate no chicanery or bamboozling. We suggest that you put nothing over on your customers, pull no wool over their eyes, and do nothing behind their backs. That way you will be able to establish a role model for what it is like to be a partner.

A partner is a collaborator in making or improving the profit of a sales relationship. Being a partner is the direct opposite of being an adversary. Partners accommodate each other. Adversaries try to finesse one another. Partners want each collaborator to win. Only one adversary can win. Adversaries take advantage of each other. Partners teach each other, help each other grow into new competence, and tie their own destinies together.

When the objective of partnering a customer is achieved through negotiating with him, the deal comes across as a *bargain*. This means that the customer perceives the value-to-price relationship of the sale to be favorable to him. No matter how much he is paying, he sees the value to be even greater. The salesman also sees the relationship as a bargain. He is able to sell at a premiun price. Each has struck a good deal with the other. It is only natural that they will want to do it again.

Out of negotiated sales transactions can come close and continuing customer partnerships that grow in mutual reward and become the backbone of a company's market.

The need for negotiated solutions for sales problems comes

from many everyday situations that occur repeatedly in every salesman's customer relationships. A customer requests technical service. The salesman must deny or delay it. Or the salesman must introduce a price increase. The customer resists it. New shipping policies, contract changes, product return requests, alterations in delivery dates, bargaining to determine the location or handling of inventory—all these situations require negotiation if the relationship is to be preserved, first of all, and enhanced for the mutual future benefit of both partners.

What is the particular magic of negotiation as a partner-building tool? For one thing, negotiation can position you and your customer as equals. As the balance of power in the relationship swings back and forth, the give and take of negotiation is the best strategy to use to bring it back to equality. Second, negotiation allows both of you to win the big ones. This is why it is called the win-win approach. Third, negotiation is a consultative process. It permits you to play the kind of selling role in which you can counsel your customer on how he can best meet his needs by applying the products and services you prescribe to solve his problems or capitalize on his opportunities. ✓These three characteristics—being equals, winning together, and setting up a counseling relationship that is devoted to problem solving—are the essence of partnership.

If you accept the argument that negotiation adds a value to the selling relationship that can improve your sales performance, and if you learn how to practice the negotiation strategies we are recommending, our experience shows that you can expect to increase your profitable sales volume by making better deals with your major customers. You will also find negotiation to be important inside your own organization to help you deal more beneficially with such internal staff functions as credit and collection, contract and price, brand and product management, engineering and manufacturing, technical service, and even your own sales and marketing management.

We ourselves are committed to negotiation as our own prime selling strategy. We use a good deal of negotiation as salesmen of our consulting services and as practicing consultants. We have also applied negotiation strategies with each other in collaborating on this book. We have written the book because we have found a good many problems with books that do not concentrate on applying principles of negotiation specifically to the sales function. A salesman cannot use the strategies of labor negotiation or international diplomacy to deceive his customer. Win-lose tactics that leave egg on the loser's face—and a yearning for revenge in his heart—have no place in building the close, continuing growth relationships on which successful salesmen must base their businesses.

We also deplore the cavalier treatment that has been given to the basic psychological principles of one-to-one interaction underlying all negotiation strategies. How, we ask, can a salesman negotiate with a customer if he lacks an essential understanding of what makes each of them perceive himself as he does or act out the role he chooses to play with the other? We consider this fundamental psychological background to be the platform for negotiation.

As you come to share the results of our thinking, keep in mind that this book represents our approach to creating a win-win relationship with you: while you win more profitable sales through negotiation, we will win the satisfaction of having counseled with you on how to expand your professional competence in this way.

Mack Hanan
James Cribbin
Howard Berrian

Contents

part one

Acquiring the Basic Background

1
How to Add Negotiation to Your Sales Strategy Mix

One way to define profit—which must be the end objective of everything you do in sales—is to think of it as your reward for customer service. Two factors make up customer service. One is *what you sell;* your products, your services, and the product-service systems that combine them. The second is *how you sell.* All other things being equal—which means the user benefits of your products and services are perceived by your customers as being more or less equaled by your competitors—how you sell can influence up to 80 percent of your sales success. If you cannot provide added value through your product line, you will have to deliver it by selling in a manner that enables your customers to win more than they can win in any other way. If you can help them achieve their objectives more surely, more profitably, and more enjoyably, you will be supplying a premium customer service.

Your reward for supplying a premium customer service is premium profit. In return for your investment in serving your customer, you win as he wins. This win-win sales strategy is what we mean by the word *negotiation.*

In a mutually profitable sales relationship where business is good and the bottom-line value of your sales volume is growing, negotiation should be the prevailing strategy in the great majority of your dealings. It will then come to trademark each of your customer relationships as a partnership for mutual

3

profit improvement. The common objective of improved profit will bind both of you. This does not mean you must both achieve the same profit from every transaction. Nor does it mean you must—or even will be able to—use negotiation as your selling strategy for every deal. Sometimes you will have to use persuasion. At other times, compromise or accommodation may be the best strategy or the only one that will work. Some situations are simply not negotiable and you will have to resolve conflict or bite the bullet and confront it. But by and large, negotiation should be your most consistent method of relating to your customers.

Why Win-Win Negotiation Is the Best Way to Sell

Win-win negotiation has five benefits over and above the values of persuasion, compromise, and accommodation. First, negotiation better serves your customer's personal and professional needs for *recognition as an individual*. In negotiating with a customer you are implicitly acknowledging his need, like yours, to have his purposes served and you are confirming that his purposes and objectives are as important to him as your goals are to you. Each of you is enhanced by the selling process. Another way to say the same thing is to state that both of you are equalized by negotiation; that is, you are positioned as peers, equally important to each other and therefore capable of becoming partners.

A second benefit of negotiation is the way it contributes to the *climate of confidence* you must create in your key-account relationships if they are to be profitable and durable. By negotiating with a customer you demonstrate that you are not out to use him merely as a means to your own ends. This enables the typical "you and me" relationship to mature into a "we and our" relationship in which the customer can have confidence that your proposals are in his own best interest as well as in yours.

Negotiation is the bargaining process preferred by salesmen who add the value of their personal applications expertise to the products and services they sell. This permits them to position themselves in an *advisory and counseling relationship* with their customers. From this position they can apply their products and services to improving customer profit. This is a third benefit of negotiation.

A fourth benefit can be derived from the *information exchange* that negotiation encourages through its give-and-take dialogs. As you negotiate, your customer is exposed to a wide range of knowledge about your company's resources, your product and service benefits, and their effects on his profitability. He also learns how well you know his business problems and opportunities. In turn, you can acquire greater in-depth knowledge about his problems, how he ranks them in order of urgency, and what political, organizational, or financial constraints may stand in the way of his taking action on them.

A fifth benefit of negotiation is its *conduciveness to establishing long-term relationships* in which you are the preferred supplier. Negotiation avoids many of the usual conflicts that often short-circuit a promising customer relationship. Unlike persuasion and compromise, which frequently contain the seeds of future conflict because they leave a residue of unfulfilled needs, negotiation can help to build a stable relationship that resists self-destruction as well as competitive inroads.

How Negotiation Differs from Persuasion, Accommodation, and Compromise

Many salesmen think they are negotiating when they are really not. They may not know the difference or care to admit it. But their customers do. You should be able to distinguish negotiation from sales strategies that are more accurately defined as persuasion, accommodation, and compromise. There is nothing wrong with using these approaches when they are appropriate. Each has its role. But they should not be mistaken for negotiation.

How Persuasion Differs from Negotiation

Persuasion is a you-win strategy. It can be a useful element of negotiation, but negotiation is not persuasion by another name. Persuasion implies the subtle imposition of your will on your customer in order to prevail over his objections and bring him around to your way of thinking. Persuasion at best can achieve only reluctant submission rather than genuine agreement. Moreover, persuasion that is used habitually can create problems:

✔ 1. It connotes that you know what is best for the customer. This is a risky assumption.

✔ 2. It makes you appear psychologically superior to your customer who then becomes suspicious that you may be manipulating him into making a purchase.

✔ 3. It implies that you are seeking to use your customer for your own ends, even when you may in fact have his best interests at heart.

✔ 4. Once persuaded does not mean always persuaded. After your customer has had time to think things over, your argument may boomerang. Thus persuasion may at times be actually counterproductive.

✔ 5. If you fail to provide your customer with countervailing arguments against later persuaders, the last persuader may get his business.

How Accommodation Differs from Negotiation

Accommodation is another one-winner strategy. Since one party must be superior, the other must be inferior. In essence, therefore, accommodation is unilateral: only the customer is expected to accommodate. The alternative is that you give in. Once having given in, you will find it harder to hold fast against accommodating your customer the next time. If you keep giving in, you may at last become so pliable that you seem more like a piece of wet spaghetti than a professional. A professional must "profess" a clear, consistent integrity. Your customer has the same mission. If either of you accommodates the other too often under pressure, both of you may find yourselves losing your sense of integrity.

How can you determine the limits within which you can accommodate safely? As Figure 1 indicates, four major constraints impinge on your freedom. The first is your convictions.

Figure 1. Constraints on free accommodation.

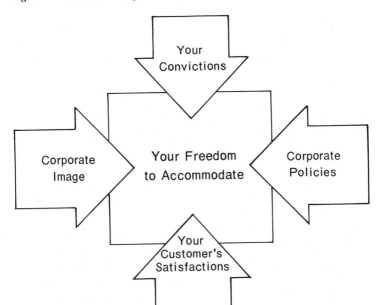

If you sacrifice them, you become a nobody. The second is your company's policies. Private deals at the company's expense have no place in negotiation. The third is your company's image. Accommodation is poor strategy if it positions your organization unfavorably in the eyes of your customers. The fourth constraint is that you must maximize the satisfactions your customers will derive from dealing with you.

How Compromise Differs from Negotiation

Compromise is a nobody-wins strategy. Even though the only way to close a sale may often require that both you and your customer give up something neither of you wants to yield, compromise carries with it at least five important limitations:

1. It may result in a solution that is acceptable to both parties but not really satisfying to either party. Each believes he has sacrificed something he really wanted to achieve. Com-

promise often gives only a temporary feeling of relief. Each party to the compromise feels cheated.

✓2. It may prompt you and your customer to be suspicious of each other. Compromise forces each party to be wary of his "opponent" and to be on guard lest he be outwitted and taken in.

✓3. It compels you and your customer to play games. You may have to start out making outlandish demands so that you have room to compromise. You may even find yourselves threatening each other. In all compromises, hidden agendas dominate the proceedings. Second-guessing and maneuvering become the accepted way of relating.

✓4. It makes agreement very hard to come by. Both parties want to get as much as possible while giving up as little as necessary. Time is wasted. Energy is consumed unproductively. Compromisers frequently alienate each other either by making insistent demands or by taking unmovable stands.

✓5. Compromise forces each party to be self-oriented, self-insistent, self-centered, and perhaps even self-indulgent. No wonder that many compromises must be renegotiated after a period of time.

When Negotiation Can Be Your Strategy of Choice

Whether you use a negotiation strategy or not is primarily determined by each individual sales situation. It is also influenced by the personal style and characteristics of the decision maker you are called on to deal with. There are two major situations where negotiation can be your strategy of choice: selling to your customers and selling internally. The second situation is often the more difficult. Figure 2 shows some typical examples of internal selling situations, and Figure 3 highlights some major customer selling situations.

Customer selling situations that call for negotiation strategies can be broken down into three types. One is *complaints*. These will usually involve problems concerning price, product performance, or company policy. The second is *requests* for spe-

Figure 2. Company selling situations.

SALESMAN/SALES MANAGER SITUATIONS
1. Assignment or realignment of territory
2. Account assignment
3. Quota establishment
4. Forecast acceptance
5. Price leverage
6. Product modification request
7. Allocation policy variance
8. New customer establishment
9. Old customer discontinuation
10. Key-account concentration
11. Staff support availability
12. Order expediting
13. Performance evaluation
14. Salary review and commission rate establishment

SALESMAN/CORPORATE STAFF SITUATIONS
1. Customer credit terms or extension from credit manager
2. Customer price reduction from price and contract manager
3. Product modification from engineering, manufacturing, product, or brand managers
4. Customer service from customer service manager

---

cial treatment or consideration in product specifications, credit, or a variety of services. The third is *innovations*. These involve the introduction of any important new information or action into your customer relationships. When a new product is to be introduced, a good deal of educational negotiation will normally be required to move it into its distribution channels and push it through to your customers and from them to the final consumers. Much of this negotiation will take the form of an information transfer between you and your customers. When you must allocate a product or a material, alter its delivery schedules or its price, or renegotiate a deal you thought you had sewed up because a new customer decision maker has joined the act, you will often find negotiation strategies to be your best bet.

You will probably find that complaints are the most difficult of the three types of customer negotiation situations. They require that you adopt defensive strategies preliminary to turning the situation around to a cooperative negotiation. On the other hand, customer requests will probably be the easiest

Figure 3. Customer selling situations.

COMPLAINTS
1. Price exceeds perceived value
2. Product fails to perform according to promise
3. Policy must be defended

REQUESTS
1. Product specifications must be customer-tailored
2. Credit must be extended
3. Service must be applied
4. Unsold merchandise or discontinued models must be returned
5. Advertising and sales promotion support must be provided
6. Market research support must be provided
7. Price concession must be granted
8. Nearby inventory must be established
9. Claims must be settled
10. Product application education must be provided

INNOVATIONS
1. New product must be introduced
2. Product must be put on allocation
3. Delivery must be speeded up or delayed
4. Price increase must be justified
5. Leasing terms must be set
6. Competitive threat must be counteracted
7. Self-manufacture must be discouraged
8. Contract must be renegotiated with a new negotiator
9. Customer policies or objectives change
10. Customer's market grows, shrinks, or changes needs

situations to convert into business opportunities. A request is a signal for help. However, because your customers have learned to expect free services or because you may want to provide free service as a sample of a larger-scale project you can charge for, you will not always be able to attach a price tag to your help.

The third type of negotiation situation—innovations—should occur most frequently in most normal sales relationships. New-product introductions and allocations, price and delivery-date changes, competitive threats or the mere threat of competitive threats, and the renegotiations made necessary by the coming and going of customer decision makers—these are the characteristic events of a dynamic customer relationship.

Negotiation is designed to preserve the stability of your customer relationships in the face of constant change. Some of these changes will be initiated by your customers. For example, they may come to you with news of competitive threats to your participation in their business. This innovation will require that you negotiate a defense until you can restore the earlier rapport. At other times, you yourself will initiate innovations that change the relationship, perhaps through a new-product introduction or a price adjustment. You will have to manage the application of cooperative negotiation strategies with your customer in all such situations.

What You Need to Know to Negotiate

To become a fluent negotiator—which means you can manage win-win sales situations with your customers on a consistent basis—you must know three things:

√ 1. The conceptual base for negotiation, which will help you understand why you and your customers act the way you do and why you play out different roles in negotiation.

2. The skill base for negotiation, which will help you understand how to ask your customer the right questions, how to listen with empathy to his answers, and how to motivate the dialog.

3. The knowledge base for negotiation, which will help you understand how your customer's decision makers decide what to buy in the context of the diverse influences operating within their organization, and how awareness of your own preconceptions, stereotypes, and hangups can help you become a positive influencer yourself.

Having fortified yourself with a working knowledge of these three bases for negotiation, you should be ready to begin negotiating with your customers by applying the process of becoming partners with them.

2
How to Acquire the
Conceptual Base for Negotiation

Mutually satisfactory negotiation rests on four conceptual foundations:

Principles of human behavior. Why do you and your customers act as you do?

Principles of perception. Why do you and your customers perceive each other as you do?

Principles of role adoption. Why do you and your customers play out different roles in negotiation?

Principles of leadership. What patterns of leadership are available to you in your role as a negotiator?

How to Use the Principles of Human Behavior

Every individual may be viewed as a fraction. We all share the same denominator of human nature and needs; on the other hand, we all have unique numerators that represent our individual differences. All negotiators share the same denominator because they are human.

What do you need to understand about human behavior? The following concepts can help you increase your negotiation effectiveness.

All customer behavior is caused, multi-motivated, goal-directed, and tension-reducing

No customer acts in a random fashion. Each usually acts on the basis of more than one motive to attain some goal that is important to him at the time, to increase his need satisfaction, or to avoid being deprived of something he now enjoys.

SALES APPLICATION

It is old hat to say that a salesman must study his customer before dealing with him. But it is more important that he be adept at analyzing him while interacting with him. What are the customer's objectives? Why is he acting as he is? What are the needs that he is trying to satisfy? What motives are driving him? Answers to these questions require hard and painstaking work. They are not arrived at by using such worn-out clichés as "Find his hot button." They involve not so much putting yourself in the customer's shoes as getting inside his head, his heart, and his gut.

SALES ILLUSTRATION

A new door-to-door salesman for cable television was having difficulty selling his service even though the monthly cost was less than $10. His primary sales points were that it gave much clearer reception and enabled the customer to view athletic events that would otherwise be unavailable. Little by little he came to the conclusion that his prospects were interested in more than clear reception and commercially untelevised athletic events. They resented the constant interruption by commercials on regular TV. They disliked paying so much to go to the movies, including the cost of a baby-sitter. Some wanted to see adult movies that had not been edited.

When his company added first-run movies to its services, the salesman concentrated not only on otherwise unavailable athletic events but also on the inconvenience of going to the movies, the cost of the movies, the cost of the baby-sitter, and the advantages of the unique and different events that were not offered by commercial or educational TV. In a short time, he was selling more than he had ever sold before. He had zeroed in on real needs. He was not selling TV but customer values.

 Whenever a customer acts, what he does makes sense to him at the time

Although it is commonly believed that man is a rational animal, in his day-to-day behavior he is likely to act more from emotion than from logic. Behavior that strikes an observant outsider as obstinate, petty, arrogant, or irrational is justified and justifiable to the individual at the time of his action, even though later he may have second thoughts or regret what he has said or done.

SALES APPLICATION

Many salesmen react to a customer's negative behavior rather than stepping back and trying to analyze why he is acting as he is. They are tempted to respond emotionally to the buyer's emotions, making it all but impossible to cope with the highly charged situation in a positive manner. It would be far better to accept and absorb, within the limits of prudence, a customer's negative flack or lack of logic. This requires self-discipline, emotional maturity, and flexibility in adapting positive behavior to deal with a customer's negative behavior.

SALES ILLUSTRATION

The newly appointed partner-in-charge of an office of one of the Big Eight accounting firms asked an important client why he had invited other firms to solicit his account. The client's response was icy: "You people are just out for the dollar, not to serve our needs." The partner's reply was genial: "Would you be willing to have lunch with me, since you have to eat anyway, and allow me to prove to you why you must stay with us?" "You'd better have something worth my while," the client retorted, "or it'll be a short lunch." The partner built his presentation around the demonstrable, measurable benefits of the firm's services. Now he bills the client more than $500,000 annually. In addition, his firm provides income-tax consultation and estate-tax planning for all top executives in the client's company.

A customer reacts to the reality he perceives, not necessarily to the reality the salesman perceives or presents

This principle lies at the heart of negotiation. Even an experienced salesman tends to assume that such things as price and specifications have the same meaning for the customer as they have for himself. A customer can use only *his* past experience, *his* needs, *his* perceptions, and *his* logic to convince himself, not those of a salesman. In this sense everyone is ego-bound.

SALES APPLICATION

A customer has the luxury of being *me*-oriented, whereas the salesman must always be *you*-oriented toward the customer. Since by nature we are all self-centered, this turnabout is one of the most difficult jobs in the world. Numerical data, charts, and graphs can be the main presentation tools in selling to a lawyer, accountant, or engineer. But they may appear "unreal" to a customer who is more people-centered than figure-sensitive. Technical jargon—or what in the government is called "federalese"—may be essential to one kind of sale but completely unsuitable to another.

Everyone has his own rules for relating and communicating with others. Each of us suffers from our trained incapacities to perceive or cope with a situation that is different from any we have dealt with before. What is "real" for lawyers is the legal real; for manufacturing managers, the production real; for engineers, the engineering real; for accountants, the financial real. A salesman who fails to appreciate this at the gut level will probably end up criticizing the ignorance or stubbornness of his customers and in the process damage his own cause.

SALES ILLUSTRATION

A computer firm sold a complex system to a company on the recommendation of that company's consultant. When it was installed it worked quite well. However, the customer thought the price was too high by some $30,000. The consultant also thought the price was too high. The computer firm sent a vice-president to look over the situation. After reviewing the facts and talking with the customer and the consultant, he agreed that the price was too high, but by only $25,000. "The check will be in the mail and on its way to you as soon as I get back to the office," he said. The "real" for the computer firm was to make a fair profit by satisfying the customer. The "real" for the customer was to have his needs satisfied, including the need to feel he was paying a fair price. The "real" for the consultant was to satisfy both parties.

✱ *The best way to understand and deal with a customer is within his frame of reference*

Intellectually, this idea seems obvious. Yet perhaps not one salesman in ten really tries to understand a customer's frame of reference. What a contrast to the answer Isaac Newton gave when he was asked the secret of his great discoveries. "I keep thinking into them," he replied simply. Being self-concerned is so essentially a part of being human that to think into reality as the other fellow perceives it, within his own frame of reference, is very difficult.

SALES APPLICATION

✱ Empathy is the ability to think *with* a customer, not *for* him; to feel *with* him, not *about* him; to move in pace *with* him, not rush *ahead of* him or lag *behind* him intellectually. A salesman should not judge, evaluate, or criticize his customers but should try to understand them within their frames of reference, however absurd these may seem to him. He should ask himself questions like these: What is the customer's frame of reference? What situation does he find himself in? Within this situation, what does he consider to be essential? Incidental? Trivial? What is crucial to him: Value? Prestige? Status? Security?

SALES ILLUSTRATION

A young salesman in a high-technology company was trying to sell one of its learning systems. After listening to about a half-hour of the presentation, the customer walked the surprised salesman courteously to the door of his office, saying: "Would you like to know why I'm escorting you out of my office? I'm the controller of this corporation. I'm not an expert in the learning process or its techniques. You know nothing about accounting and finance. Therefore, we cannot do business." The salesman read up on corporate finance, accepted tutoring from financial executives in his own company, and returned to win over the controller with a presentation based on cost justification and profit improvement. Aided by the controller's support, the salesman sold his learning systems to the entire corporation.

The only things a customer really understands are those he has experienced, and the only things to which he will make a commitment are those in which he has been involved and to which he has contributed

Let's take an example. Imagine that you are in a college class of about 150 students. The professor is lecturing to them from a platform three feet higher than they are. The students spend most of their time listening and taking notes. What do you think the teacher is trying to get across? He is lecturing on the nature of democracy while being actively autocratic. The students are passively dependent. How much of what they learn about democracy will they be able to apply in their daily behavior? One signer of the Declaration of Independence declared that he preferred a decision that was only 50 percent technically sound but that people would embrace with 90 percent enthusiasm over a decision that was 90 percent technically correct but that people would embrace with only 50 percent enthusiasm. *No relationship can endure that satisfies the needs of only one of the parties.*

SALES APPLICATION

Aristotle once commented that every vice stems from either an excess or a deficiency of a virtue. Salesmen are always in danger of excess or deficiency. The passive ordertaker and the "verbal insert" who could be replaced by a well-written letter are in danger of being too passive. They allow a customer to dictate the terms of the relationship. On the other hand, salesmen who are overly aggressive, manipulative, or persuasive are in danger of being perceived as too assertive. They may come on too strong, talk too much, and seek to dominate the customer. Even the problem-solving and expert-resource types of salesmen may run into this difficulty if they seek to impose their solutions on a customer. No one likes to be put in a passive or defensive position.

SALES ILLUSTRATION

An insurance salesman was trying to sell a life insurance policy to a college teacher. Even though the salesman was an old friend of the prospect, he failed to make the sale. It went to a perfect stranger. What was wrong? The salesman took the prospect to a fine lunch. He tried to dazzle him with figures and charts that were too simplistic for the prospect, who had taught statistics for some ten years. He tried to sell the sizzle rather than the steak.

The prospect later told the salesman why the sale had gone to a competitor. "I blew it!" the salesman exclaimed. "I forgot you taught statistics. I forgot you had only a limited amount of money to invest. You see, I've been selling mostly to M.D.s. Their time is limited. They know little and care less about how much the insurance will cost. They rarely examine figures carefully. I never really gave you a chance to explain what you had in mind, did I?"

A year later, the salesman called to say that he had sold over 30 percent of his new policy business to teachers. "They're an opinionated group who like to talk, aren't they?" he commented. "You can't sell them by shoving it down their throats."

New experiences are internalized in each customer's own unique way

When a customer encounters a new experience—and this occurs frequently in the negotiation process—he predictably will do one of five things:

1. He will integrate it with his past experience easily because it is pleasant and compatible.
2. He will reject it totally because the new experience is too threatening.
3. He will isolate it from what he is accustomed to, treating the new experience as an exception, so that he can continue to think and act customarily.
4. He will distort the new experience to make it fit in with his past experience.

5. He will change his old ways of thinking and acting in order to conform to the new reality.

One of the major challenges faced by every salesman who uses negotiation is to teach his customers how to relate to him in win-win situations. The vast majority of customers are used to win-lose interactions with salesmen. If the salesman wins, they assume they must lose something. That both the salesman and the customer are winners is an unheard-of experience for them. At the outset of converting them to win-win situations, you'll most likely find them at best skeptical and at worst cynical. This is true despite the fact that they operate on a win-win basis as a matter of course with their doctors, lawyers, clergymen, and some of their accountants.

SALES APPLICATION
Most customers have had more than their fair share of experience in fending off manipulative, self-serving salesmen who have sought only to use and abuse them. Because of their hard-earned preconceptions, helping customers enter a win-win relationship takes time, persistent effort, and considerable self-reeducation.

SALES ILLUSTRATION
After trying on a wide variety of suits, a customer selected the best of the lot without enthusiasm. Whereupon the salesman said, ''Sir, if you really want to buy this suit, I'll sell it to you. But frankly, I don't think it looks that good on you. I can get a suit that I think you'll like much more than this one, in your size, from one of our other stores. If you can wait a few days, I'll call you as soon as it comes in.'' The salesman created a win-win situation by risking loss of the sale. The result was that the customer waited and got a suit that truly pleased him. A mutually profitable relationship was established and has held fast for over 15 years because the customer discovered a salesman who acted as his partner.

How to Use the Principles of Perception

In sales negotiation, four factors are paramount: substance, strategies, interaction, and manner. Successful negotiation hinges on your ability to perceive others accurately and to help them perceive you as you prefer to be seen. All interpersonal actions and reactions stem from mutual perceptions and misperceptions. Let's examine the case of two men who have held the same job with quite different results.

Robert Wagner and John Lindsay were both mayors of New York City. One got along well with the municipal unions and gave them less. The other gave them much more and had a terrible time with them. Why? The union leaders perceived Wagner as a friend who appeared at their christenings, weddings, and bar mitzvahs. Lindsay was perceived as a haughty, aloof patrician who was "too good" for the working class. Whether these perceptions were true or false matters little. The fact is that union-management relations and costs to the city have been enormously different as a result.

Nothing is so simple, and yet so complex, as the process of perception. Simply put, it is the way we get to know "what is out there." Actually, it is a complicated form of interaction between two or more people. Whenever a salesman deals with a customer, as Figure 4 shows, five different interactions can take place whether either party is aware of it or not.

1. The salesman brings with him *an image of himself* in customer relationships. He also has *an image of the customer*. These images must be as accurate and precise as possible. Otherwise negotiation will be unproductive. It may even be counterproductive.

EXAMPLES

One salesman perceives himself as inadequate and fearful of his customer. He sees the customer as far more intelligent than he is. This salesman is off to a terrible start and will probably not sell anything, and he may well earn the customer's contempt. Another salesman sees himself as an expert who knows everything. He sees his customer as slow and not too bright. Inevitably, this salesman will relate to the customer in a condescending and patronizing manner, thus incurring his resentment and resistance.

2. The customer brings with him *an image of himself* in sales relationships. He also has *an image of the salesman*.

Figure 4. The ten negotiating images.

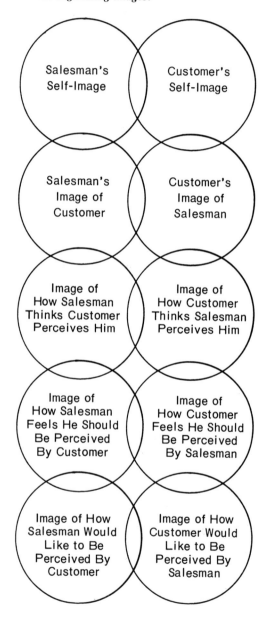

Unlike the salesman's need to be precise in his perceptions, it is not necessary that the customer's images be accurate. They are psychological "givens" of the customer, and for better or worse the salesman will have to deal with them.

EXAMPLES

One customer perceives the salesman as a slick conniver intent on making a sale in any way he can. It would be just as easy, of course, for the customer to perceive the salesman as a consultative helpmate intent on supporting the customer's needs and goals. Another customer sees himself as the one who holds the upper hand because he can give or withhold an order. He sees the salesman as someone who needs his business and can therefore be toyed with. It would be just as easy for the customer to be educated to see himself in need of help and to see the salesman as the one person who is most competent and willing to assist him.

3. A salesman has *an image of how he thinks his customer perceives him.* Naturally, the customer has *an image of how he thinks the salesman perceives him.* If both these images are incorrect, neither of the parties will be able to react to the real, live person in front of him. The salesman will respond to an image the customer does not admit to while the customer may respond to an image the salesman does not admit to. Here is where sales are lost.

EXAMPLES

One salesman *thinks* his customer perceives him as a sharp, assertive, knowledgeable expert who is trying to help the customer make the best possible choices. If he acts out this role, selling is easy. But another salesman *thinks* the customer perceives him as sharp and assertive despite the fact that the customer actually perceives him as pushy, slick, and overly aggressive. Trouble here is unavoidable; the perceptions of the two parties are in conflict and therefore their behavior will clash.

Every salesman must realize that what matters is not only how each party perceives the other. How each *thinks* the other perceives him has an important bearing on the success or failure of their negotiations.

4. Each salesman and each customer has *his own unique image of how he expects to be perceived and treated.* These images can be based on fact, fancy, or a mixture of the two. Treating a customer the way he *feels* he ought to be treated is one of the surest ways of winning his goodwill.

EXAMPLES

A salesman for a prestigious company may believe he should be treated with an unusual amount of deference. If his customer feels that the salesman should be given credit for an uncommon degree of knowledge of the matter under discussion, the two will make a good working team. But if the same salesman is involved with a customer who is domineering, arrogant, and inclined to grind salesmen into the linoleum, few sales will be made unless the salesman is an expert at biting his tongue and controlling his temper. The reverse set of conditions can easily be imagined with even more dismal results.

Every customer is a unique individual with his own set of rules for interacting with salesmen. He has certain expectations about how he should treat salesmen and, more importantly, how they should behave toward him. When these expectations are violated, he will become alienated.

5. Every salesman and every customer has *his own image of how he would like to be perceived and treated,* whether he merits such treatment or not. To the extent that conditions permit, the perceptive salesman goes out of his way to negotiate with his customer in the same manner as he would prefer to be treated.

EXAMPLES

A customer sees himself as an expert in a subject under consideration. He likes to be consulted and to have things cleared through him before a decision is made, and he likes others to acknowledge his expertise. A salesman would be wise to consult with him, if possible, even though the customer is in fact not really expert or may even be operating on the basis of outdated knowledge. This is not to suggest that the salesman must become a hypocrite just to make a sale. He can accommodate the customer within the limits of his convictions while at the same time helping the customer to update his knowledge. A salesman who would like to be treated as a consultative problem solver goes out of his way to make his customer more successful. If the customer feels no obligation to treat him in this manner, the salesman may have to put his own needs in a secondary position. Moreover, he must be on guard lest his resentment at not being treated "properly" subtly damage the sales relationship.

The interacting images of salesmen and their customers are really the entities that do business with one another in sales negotiation. They show how complex perception is. What can we say we know regarding perception?

How a salesman perceives and reacts to a customer is a function of how the customer perceives and responds to the salesman

The founder of IBM used to insist that his salesmen talk to the customer's top man. He also insisted that they would have a chance to do so only if they dressed and conducted themselves acceptably to this level. In contrast, a poorly styled salesman tempts customers to treat him in a trivial and offhand manner.

Likes, not opposites, generally attract each other

Aggression tends to stimulate aggression. A helping attitude triggers a helping attitude. Openness is usually matched by openness. A hard-selling salesman, sometimes without realizing it, prompts his customers to be defensive and to play games with him.

First impressions tend to be lasting and erroneous

A salesman who is diffident, lacking in self-assurance, and defensive projects a poor social image and attracts negative reactions from customers. On the other hand, a salesman who initially projects self-assurance had better be able to sustain it throughout a relationship. Otherwise, he will mislead the customer until he fizzles out like a Roman candle.

Perception plays a gating and steering function that also links traits that may not even be present

A salesman who makes a positive initial impact makes it easy for customers to perceive his good attributes. He creates in them a mind-set that allows them to be insensitive to his weaknesses. This occurs because we all have our own ideas of what characteristics should go together. It is difficult to perceive a generous and likable salesman as also being dishonest. This, of course, is one of the main strengths of the con man. Because he is likable and seemingly solicitous, it is almost second nature to perceive him as being honest and trustworthy even when we have hard evidence that he does not possess these qualities.

Perception is a personalized process

Salesmen and customers alike have their own individual rules for perceiving others, however valid or ridiculous they may appear to be. Intellectual, physical, and personality traits that impress one customer may very well leave another unmoved, or even provoke a negative reaction in him.

We perceive what we expect or need to perceive

Everyone tends to see what he looks for. If a customer likes a salesman and wants to think well of him, he will focus on the traits that make it easy to retain his liking for him. He will be more or less blind to qualities that might force him to change his liking. The reverse is also true. Moreover, perception is need-fulfilling. We tend to see mirages in the desert because they satisfy our dominant needs of the moment.

Perception is often a self-fulfilling prophecy

On the basis of inadequate evidence, a customer may misinterpret a salesman's deliberateness as a lack of intellectual acumen. The customer will thereafter be hypersensitive to anything that tends to confirm this initial and inaccurate perception while filtering out all contrary evidence. He will thus end up by saying, "He *is* slow. I was right all along."

A way of perceiving is a way of not perceiving

Both salesmen and customers can suffer from the same problem of channel overload. There are just too many signals from each other to attend to, sort out, and integrate. According to the law of perceptional parsimony, each person focuses on those cues that he feels will give him the best possible understanding. Thus, the salesman may concentrate on the fact that the customer is gregarious and likable but fail to perceive that he is also devious and manipulative. Or he may see that the customer drives a hard bargain but fail to perceive that he is also fair and honest.

Perception is unified and not discrete

Through our perceptions, we get a picture of the total person, however accurate or imprecise it may be. In order to act, we need a stable, generalized view of him. To obtain this integrated picture, we may blur inconsistencies and block out contradictory evidence. If the salesman likes the customer, he will tend to overestimate the ways in which the two of them are similar. If he dislikes the customer, he will tend to overemphasize the ways in which they are different. One pitfall can be as dangerous as the other.

Perception can be an exercise in projection

Projection is an ego-protecting mechanism. It takes one of two forms. A salesman may blame the customer for what is really the salesman's fault. The customer who asks penetrating questions may be perceived as a nit-picker simply because the salesman did not do his homework and does not have the answers. The second form of projection is more pernicious. It involves attributing our own failings to others. The salesman who is a schemer will tend to see the customer as more calculating than he actually is. To do otherwise would burden him with a load of guilt he would not care to carry.

The ability to perceive others is a complex skill

Even Sigmund Freud was not a good judge of people with whom he was emotionally involved. The same is true of all of us. Emotions, feelings, attitudes, preferences, and aversions distort our perceptions of others. "Reading" others accurately is one of the most demanding skills. Customers send out so many cues that the average salesman is capable of focusing only on some of them. At times we look for the wrong qualities. Even doing our level best, it is difficult to sort the substantive from the superficial and to sift genuine qualities from artificial qualities in others.

Self-insight makes it easier to perceive others as they really are

A salesman who understands his own strengths and weaknesses is better able to perceive customers as they are. If he is self-aware and secure in himself, he creates a climate of confidence that makes it easy for his customers to respond naturally and without contrived defenses. Moreover, self-insight prevents a salesman from passing extreme judgments on his customers. The Socratic injunction, "Know thyself," is still the first step to a clear perception of others.

How to Make the Most of the Roles that Customers Adopt

A major problem in negotiation that is rarely given sufficient attention is how to cope with the roles that customers adopt to achieve their objectives. Union negotiators assume that their role is to get as much as they can. Management negotiators assume that their role is to fight off the union while yielding as little as possible.

Like perception, the problem of role adoption in negotiation is quite complicated. There are five major kinds of roles and role relationships.

1. Self-Perceived Role

Every customer approaches his job with a pretty clear notion of the kinds of behavior he expects to engage in and those he does not see himself performing. Both the salesman and the customer have their unique self-defined roles in negotiation. Other things being equal, each will strive mightily to carry out his role in spite of what the other does or even in spite of antagonistic feedback he may receive.

NEGATIVE EXAMPLE

A persuasive salesman sees his role as winning the customer over to his viewpoint by a forceful presentation, by overwhelming any objections the customer may have, and by impelling him to buy. The customer, however, sees his role in terms of getting the best deal possible by beating the salesman down and outwitting him. The result of these self-perceived roles is usually a power struggle in which the more powerful of the two will win. This is a win-lose relationship.

POSITIVE EXAMPLE

A consultative salesman sees his role as helping customers to satisfy their needs. The customer sees his role as getting the best possible product or service benefits from a reliable, straight-dealing company while paying a price that is in keeping with such value. These assumptions form the basis of a win-win relationship.

2. Sent Role

Both the salesman and the customer must take into account and respond to complex forces within their respective organizations. Sent roles represent behavior that superiors and associates expect of a salesman or a customer. Sent roles are imposed roles.

EXAMPLE

A salesman has a key account that grosses $1 million a year. The role sent him by his company is that under no condition is he to lose this account. He will put this firm at the top of his priorities. He will cultivate it in every way he can. He will service it at the expense of lesser accounts. He will make every effort to retain its goodwill, even if he must squander most of the profit on the account to do so.

3. Expected Role

Every customer has his own idea of how he expects a salesman to act toward him. To a lesser extent, the salesman has his own idea of how a customer should act toward him. When these expected roles are compatible, win-win negotiation can take place. When they are in conflict, negotiation will be rocky.

EXAMPLE

A salesman expects his customer to be stimulated by the offering he presents: his products or services, price, specifications, and so on. His model of negotiation is that of Pavlov (the salesman) and his dogs (the customers). The customer, however, has different role expectations of the salesman. He expects the salesman to be a profit planner, a problem solver, an expert resource, and a need satisfier, in addition to being of help in getting the customer the maximum value from each negotiation. No sale can be made under these conditions unless the salesman is perceptive enough to pick up his customer's cues and flexible enough to alter his strategies of negotiation.

4. Role Ambiguity

Role ambiguity occurs when a customer or salesman does not know for certain how he should behave or what is the most appropriate behavior. The simplest illustration is the newly appointed sales manager who was a hotshot salesman but has had no training or experience in sales management. Role ambiguity is hurtful. No one can lead another while being unsure of what he himself should do. No one can engender confidence in another when he himself lacks self-assurance.

EXAMPLE

A customer plays cat and mouse with the salesman or is domineering and demeaning while venting his venom on the vulnerable salesman. To make the sale, should the salesman reciprocate with cat-and-mouse strategies of his own or ignore the game and bring the customer back to the main points at issue? Should he disregard the emotionalism and stick to the realities of the situation? Should he let the customer know he is not his whipping boy? The most appropriate response may be to pick up his hat and leave, indicating through body language that he will once again talk business when the customer is willing to act like a mature adult.

5. Role Conflicts

Role conflicts usually come in one of three forms: (1) intrasender, (2) intersender, and (3) person-role. A conflict is not merely frustration. Frustration is a blocking that can usually be unblocked. Conflict is the inability to attain two or more contradictory objectives simultaneously or to satisfy opposed needs or wants. Conflict is always a painful experience.

Intrasender conflict. This type of conflict occurs when a person demands that you satisfy contrary expectations simultaneously. Your manager may give you what are really contradictory orders: You must generate a lot of new business, but you must also satisfactorily service all the customers you now have, even those that are marginal and account for very little of your overall sales.

EXAMPLE: A customer insists that you provide him with more and better service but will not accept a price increase for these added values.

Intersender conflict. This type of conflict is the equivalent of being caught between the devil and the deep blue sea. It occurs when two people who are important to you require that you carry out mutually exclusive behavior.

EXAMPLE: A customer demands that he receive special consideration in regard to delivery, price reduction, credit extension, or adjustment of the basic specifications of your product or service. He threatens that he will otherwise take his business elsewhere. On the other hand, your sales or credit manager maintains that there is no way these things can be done. Even so, you are expected to retain the customer.

Person-role conflict. This type of conflict arises when a salesman is compelled to do something that is contrary to his personal values and convictions.

EXAMPLE: In some industries, bidding collusion among suppliers is periodically uncovered. Some men refuse to go along with this arrangement. They stick by what they think is the right thing to do. Others sacrifice their convictions to carry out their expected roles.

To paraphrase Shakespeare, during negotiation the players adopt many roles. The salesman who is not sensitive to the fact that a customer is adopting or shifting roles—and cannot ascertain for what reasons—or who is unable to shift his own role to accommodate the feedback he gets from the customer, will make very few sales. To negotiate successfully, a salesman must know:

1. What role a customer is playing at the moment and for what reasons. Is it self-prescribed or other-imposed?
2. What role the salesman is adopting and for what reasons. What is it earning for him positively and negatively?
3. What role the salesman can adopt to improve his position in the negotiation.
4. What the salesman can do to help the customer adopt a different role that will be more productive.

How to Take a Leadership Role in Negotiation

Leadership is the process of influencing commitment. You become a leader when your customers allow you to influence them. There are two basic types of leadership patterns, negative and positive. Figure 5 shows four negative patterns: aggressive, manipulative, compromising, and persuasive. A salesman who applies his leadership by aggressively confronting his customers or by selfishly manipulating their needs may still make many sales, but he will be unlikely to make a partnership of his sales relationships.

In Figure 6, three positive leadership patterns are shown: a stimulus-response pattern, a bargaining pattern, and an integrative pattern. These patterns are conducive to creating win-win partnerships.

Figure 5. Negative leadership patterns.

VARIABLE	AGGRESSIVE PATTERN	MANIPULATIVE PATTERN	COMPROMISING PATTERN	PERSUASIVE PATTERN
Right to lead	Personal strength	Superior shrewdness	Ability to temporize	Fluent cleverness
Usual strategy	Force the customer	Outwit the customer	Yield to the customer	Play on the customer's likes and dislikes
Self-prescribed role	Overwhelm the customer	Con the customer	Please the customer at any cost	Seduce the customer
Role sent to the customer	Submit	Be outmaneuvered	Press as hard as possible	Gladly submit to the salesman's "sweet talk"
Reaction of the customer	Resentment	Defensiveness	Contempt	Wariness
Achievement orientation	To make a sale through conquest	To make a sale by pulling the wool over the customer's eyes	To make a sale at any price	To make a sale by winning over the customer
Communication	Self-insistent	Devious	Appeasing	Charming
Motivation method	Push-drive intimidation	Trickery	Receptive yielding	Bribery—selling the sizzle
Decision-making process	Unilateral—"on my terms"	Unilateral—seductive	Unilateral—"on the customer's terms"	Emotional enthusiasm without conviction
Salesman's needs met	Dominance through control	Dominance through dependence and cleverness	Dominance through dependence	Dominance by winning customer agreement
Customer's needs met	Deference	Dependence	Dominance	Pseudosecurity and friendship
Time span of the relationship	Short term—future rebellion	Short term—future avoidance	Short term—loss of mutual respect	Short term—reluctance to be taken twice

Figure 6. Positive leadership patterns.

VARIABLE	STIMULUS-RESPONSE PATTERN (AIDA)	BARGAINING PATTERN	INTEGRATIVE PATTERN
Right to lead	Skill in drawing desired responses from the customer	Skill in making trade-offs that injure neither party seriously	Skill in building collaboration
Usual strategy	Get the customer's attention, arouse interest, create desire, get action	Press for all he can get, adjusting to the customer's pressures when necessary	Work with the customer to bring about an integration of their separate needs and goals
Self-prescribed role	Induce the customer to buy by skillfully drawing him out and pulling him along	Adjust to the customer as much as he must to attain his goals; the customer's goals are secondary	Build a lasting and profitable relationship based on mutual trust
Role sent to the customer	Respond as expected to the stimuli received	Let the salesman know the areas in which accommodation is necessary	Cooperate with the salesman in order to build a mutually satisfying relationship
Reaction of the customer	A responder, not a participant; at times, a feeling of being manipulated	An attitude of guarded give and take	An attitude of partnership in a joint venture
Achievement orientation	To overcome the customer's resistance and get him to buy	To get the best deal possible while making as few adjustments as necessary	To make sure that both succeed optimally, neither succeeding at the other's expense

Communication pattern	Stimulus-response salesman keeps the initiative and control	Basically honest but geared more to the salesman's needs than the customer's	Free and open; geared to the balanced attainment of the goals of both parties
Motivation method	Positive reinforcement of correct responses; negative reinforcement of incorrect responses	Give-and-take reward system	Sharing of mutual success
Decision-making process	Customer is brought to the decision desired by the salesman	Trading off with the customer so that the salesman can get him to agree	Joint decision making; willingness to share leadership according to competence
Salesman's needs met	Dominance, control, and achievement in causing the customer to buy	Achievement in getting the sale while trading off as little as possible	Achievement in attaining the goals of both parties
Customer's needs met	Dependence, security, social achievement	Dominance, security, social autonomy, recognition achievement	Consultation, participation, teamwork, security, social achievement
Time span of the relationship	Brief, especially if the customer realized that he is a mere responder	Uncertain, depending on how well the trade-offs help the customer to attain his objectives	Longterm—increased satisfaction for both parties with their win-win relationship

3
How to Acquire the
Skill Base for Negotiation

The aim of sales negotiation is to obtain mutually profitable sales agreements. This is the essence of a win-win relationship. To achieve agreements, four skills are essential: (1) the ability to communicate with impact, (2) the ability to ask the right questions, (3) the ability to listen with empathy, and (4) the ability to motivate.

How to Communicate with Impact

Rousseau once said, "Man is like a rabbit. You must catch him by his ears." Communication is a two-way interaction in which messages are accepted and acted upon or rejected and ignored. How can you communicate with impact?

Let's examine what can happen when a salesman tries to communicate with a customer. The salesman applies "communication theory." The customer's reactions illustrate what often occurs when theory meets reality.

THE SALESMAN'S APPLICATION OF COMMUNICATION THEORY	THE CUSTOMER'S REACTIONS
Has a need or desire to interact with the customer	May or may not want to listen to the salesman

Perceives the situation and his relationship with the customer from his viewpoint	Perceives the situation and his relationship with the salesman from his viewpoint
Structures the objectives he wants to attain	May agree with the salesman's objectives but is sure to have his own personal "agenda"
Composes his message	May or may not be open to the salesman's message
Encodes the message in terms that he thinks the customer will accept	May or may not be comfortable with the salesman's encoding process
Sends the message to the customer as clearly and convincingly as possible	Receives the message but may be inattentive, distracted, or more concerned with what he wants to say in return
Tries to ensure that the customer understands and accepts the message	May or may not accept the message, or may decode it incorrectly, distort it, misinterpret certain crucial parts, or be offended by its tone or content
Tries to get the customer to agree with him, to feel as he does, and to behave appropriately	May disagree, resist, or become emotionally negative
Seeks to get feedback from the customer about how well he has reached him	May or may not give the salesman honest feedback or may deliberately mislead him

How to Avoid "Dialogs of the Deaf"

When the communication process goes wrong, static or noise results. Neither communicator hears the other. They play a semantic Ping-Pong game in which words, not meanings, are exchanged. Feelings may be expressed but are rarely shared. One of the most discouraging experiences in negotiation is the sense of not being understood. Although there are a great many reasons why a salesman's communication with customers can go awry, the following dozen are among the most common:

☐ The salesman thinks the meaning of the communication is in himself. It is not. Meaning is always in the customer.

☐ He takes for granted that the customer's frame of reference is similar to his own. This is rarely the case in negotiation.

☐ He assumes the words he uses mean the same to the customer as to him.

☐ He operates on the premise that what he has to say includes all that is worth saying.

☐ He forgets that communication is a shared experience.

☐ If static occurs, he imagines that it stems primarily from disagreement about clearly defined courses of action. More often than not, disagreement arises from different perceptions of the same situation.

☐ Apparent understanding can also create later noise. Both parties may assume they are on the same frequency only to discover that their lines are badly crossed.

☐ The salesman may assume he is communicating whenever he speaks. In truth, he communicates only when a customer accepts, understands, and is influenced by his words.

☐ He fancies that communication is principally a matter of saying the right thing in the right way. This is important but not paramount. Studies have shown that only about 7 percent of face-to-face communication is accomplished by words. Vocal intonation and inflection account for another 38 percent while facial expression and body language account for the remaining 55 percent.

☐ He assumes the customer is giving him his undivided attention. Because most attention is really selective inattention, this rarely happens. The customer listens to what he finds real for him.

☐ The salesman fails to realize that communication is a dialog and not a process of unilateral bludgeoning.

☐ He may concentrate so hard on the meaning of what he says that he disregards the emotional impact he is making.

Since it takes two to tango, many of these same causes of noise may have their origins in the customer.

How to Make Your Communications More Effective

There is a basic group of skills that can help make your communications with your customer more effective:

☐ During negotiation, bear in mind that communication is a human transaction. People impact on people.

☐ Know precisely what you want to achieve but be mindful of how the customer is likely to interpret and react to your objectives. Be sensitive to his contrary or conflicting objectives.

☐ Before you begin to communicate, take time to discover what arouses the customer's enthusiasm, what stirs his interest, what leaves him cold and indifferent, what annoys him and makes him touchy, and where his blind spots are.

☐ Always communicate something of value as the customer defines what is valuable.

☐ Remember that the customer always has two questions in his mind: "How will this negotiation affect me?" and "What's in it for me?"

☐ Remind yourself that manner is often more important than meaning in face-to-face communication. If a customer does not buy your manner, he will probably not buy your meaning.

☐ When you communicate with a customer, make sure you are only 85 percent infallible. It is difficult for a customer to relate to a salesman who knows everything.

☐ Since negotiation is a dialog, you must allow ample time for the customer to "get his oar in."

☐ Be conscious that all of you is communicating: your words, body posture, facial expressions, tone of voice, and inflections.

☐ Be sensitive to the impact of expressive silence in communication.

☐ Try to anticipate the most probable reception for your communication.

☐ Try to create a climate of acceptance for what you say even when the customer may not want to hear it.

☐ Know to what extent, and for what reasons, the customer respects you.

☐ Be aware of the customer's biases. Be equally sensitive to your own preferences and aversions.

☐ Remember that the language of feelings and emotions is often far more compelling than the language of the intellect.

☐ Choose key words according to their expected brain, heart, and gut impact.

☐ Be mindful of the relationship that exists between you and your customer. Stay within it. Do not presume on the relationship.

☐ An effective communicator is a good translator. He translates what he considers important into terms the customer will accept, will understand within his frame of reference, and will find motivating.

How to Ask the Right Questions

Every salesman needs two kinds of negotiating feedback from his customer: *reactions* to help him keep the dialog progressing and *cues* that assure him he is getting through to the customer and that can guide him in deciding what he should say next. These reactions and cues can be ascertained largely by the skillful use of questions.

A question is a two-edged sword. If it is positive, it can help reveal how the customer is thinking and feeling. If it is negative, it can make the customer uneasy or put him on the defensive. Whereas the salesman directly reveals very little of himself in his questioning, he requests that the customer not only reveal himself but supply important information without knowing just how the salesman will use this information. Before considering some of the major types of negotiating questions, here are some guidelines:

☐ Questions should represent an attempt to reach agreement. They should not be impudent invasions of privacy.

☐ Questions should not make the customer uncomfortable or cause him anxiety.

☐ Questions should help both parties. They are not meant to be manipulative.

☐ Questions should be phrased to create a climate of cooperation by motivating the customer to give candid answers.

☐ Questions should not be tricky, emotionally loaded, devious, embarrassing, double-barreled, or petty.

☐ Questions should be appropriate to the situation.

☐ Questions should be compatible with the client's personality and frame of mind.

☐ Questions should be designed to achieve an objective, not just to elicit an answer.

☐ Questions should build on each other.

☐ Questions should be characterized by civility and respect for the customer.

The "right" questions can be gathered together under seven classifications.

Implementation questions. These are direct questions that every newspaper reporter tries to answer in the first paragraph of his story in order to implement his communication: Who? What? Where? When? How? Why?

Confirming questions. The purpose of questions of this sort is twofold: to ensure that the salesman and his customer are in agreement, and to direct the customer's attention to new areas in the hope of getting added commitment from him. Confirming questions are often phrased somewhat as follows: "Then we're agreed that. . . . Aren't we?" Or, "We're both of the opinion that this is the way to go, right?" Or, "It's settled, then, that we'll provide these additional services and you'll accept our small price increase?"

Nondirective questions. These questions are open-ended in the sense that they usually cannot be answered with a simple yes or no. They open up the customer by impelling him to discuss a matter further. By priming the customer's vocal cords, the salesman can pick up cues as to just how he should proceed. Here are several examples of nondirective questions. "What happened then?" "What might have been the cause-and-effect relationship?" "Suppose this could be done, how would you feel then?" "Is anyone likely to veto your decision?" "Was there a reason for the change?" "Was anybody's big toe stepped on?"

Restatement-of-content questions. Whenever a customer has been talking for a while, it is advisable to let him know he is not "talking to a wall." One way to do this is to restate as precisely as possible what he has just said. This can reassure him and stimulate him to continue. You might put such a restatement question this way: "As I understand your position, you'd like to use our product but you think the price is still a bit out of line. Is that it?" Or, "You and I are convinced, but am I right in concluding that the division manager is the one who hasn't yet bought our idea?" Or, "Is your problem that it may be hard to justify this expenditure when the company is on a cost reduction kick?"

If you restate the intellectual content of a customer's comments accurately, the feedback will be instantaneous: "That's it exactly." Or, "Yes, and let me tell you something else." Or some similar affirmative expression. However, if your restatement is incorrect, the feedback will be equally quick: "No, that's not what I mean." Or, "That's only a small part of the problem." Or some such negative statement.

Reflection-of-feeling questions. These questions aim to mirror as exactly as possible a feeling or emotion a customer has expressed. You can do this by asking: "Am I right in thinking that lately you've been a little disappointed with the service you've been getting?" Or, "Could it be that it's the uncertainty that's bothering you? Would you feel better if I assure you that the entire problem will be cleared up within the week?"

Redirected questions. There are times when the best way to answer a question is to redirect it to the customer. "That's an interesting question; I'm glad you brought it up. Based on your experience, how might we go about coping with this situation?" Or, "That's something we'll have to monitor very carefully from the outset. How do you think we should go about it?" Or, "Before I answer your question, would you mind describing briefly what characteristics a good solution should have?"

Keep-it-moving questions. The purpose of many questions is to get the customer talking. At times, a single word, a phrase, a facial expression, a change in your physical position, or even silence can help you "ask" a question. An "Uh-huh?" or "Is that so?" can do this. When used properly, these questions let the customer know you are paying attention to him without interrupting his flow of thought or distracting him.

Every question in a negotiation should have a specific purpose. Let's explore a variety of questions that can be asked and set a purpose for each.

To check understanding: "You say you like our product but think our price is a bit out of line?"

To establish reasons: "We realize that we've usually received only 20 percent of your business in the past. Why is that?"

To obtain reaction: "Well, that's our proposal. I honestly feel it's in your best interests. What do you think?"

To obtain suggestions: "You say that, with some modifications, the system we propose might work well for you. How do you think we might adapt it to meet your specific requirements?"

To act as devil's advocate: "If you really want the lower-price equipment, we'll supply it and assure you that it'll meet your present needs. But with your plans for growth and expansion, I doubt that it'll meet your needs for the future. What do you think?"

To catch attention: "Suppose I can prove to you that in spite of its initial higher cost, this equipment will be less expensive on the basis of day-to-day use, maintenance, and training requirements. Would you be willing to explore the long-term benefits and overall costs?"

To elicit information: "I've learned a good deal about your operations. Obviously, you know far more. What profit opportunities and problems are you looking ahead to over the next year or so?"

To give data: "Did you know all the ways our technical support group will work with your people on the installation of this equipment, and will help them monitor it until you're satisfied that it's on stream?"

To bring a sale to a conclusion: "We've covered all the points you said are important to you. The only remaining step is for me to write up the contract to assure you of early delivery."

To keep contact: "You say you want some time to think over the proposal. What would you say to my calling you on Monday so that we can get back together and wrap things up?"

To find out who has power to help or hinder: "I know the equipment will be located in your department and managed by your people. Are there any other managers or departments whose operations will be affected?"

To follow up: "Would you have any objection to my calling on you every week after our equipment is installed in order to make sure it's performing exactly the way we both want it to?"

To emphasize ethical considerations: "I can understand that what you propose might solve your problem. But how fair would it be to our other customers if we begin to make such broad special exceptions?"

To secure opinions: "Suppose we take your present equipment as a trade-in and credit you against the purchase of our new and much more efficient model. What's your reaction to this option?"

To arouse discussion: "Suppose I assure you this product will do not only everything you say you want but even more. Would you be willing to discuss it for a few minutes?"

To discover intensity of feeling: "I know that nobody likes a price increase. But have you calculated the added values you'll receive for it?"

To determine resistance: "Sounds too good to be true? What parts of the proposal seem to offer you too much value?"

To determine readiness to move ahead: "Are we agreed, then, that our system will meet your needs best and that the value is right? What's the next step we should discuss?"

To ferret out doubts: "Our system works for other firms in your line of business. I'm convinced it'll be good for you. But it's even more important that you be convinced. Are there any loose ends we haven't covered?"

To obtain evaluation: "Knowing the realities that you and your people must cope with, to what extent do you think this service will increase your overall operating efficiency? Where do you think it may not make enough of a contribution?"

To draw on past experience: "You've had a great deal of experience in introducing new product lines like this. What's been your experience regarding the problems of being first?"

To discover the source· "You said we have the reputation of servicing our larger customers thoroughly, but at times we seem to be less concerned about smaller customers. If this were really true, our smaller customers would never become our larger customers. I'd be interested in learning just how you got this idea."

To focus attention: "We've been talking about the general advantages of the services we offer. From where you sit, what would you say is the greatest benefit you yourself would derive?"

To obtain feedback: "We've been your major supplier for more than five years. How do you feel we might be of even greater service to you over the next five years?"

To stimulate reflective thinking: "We've been discussing sev-

eral problems. But have we been talking about causes
or merely symptoms? What would you say is the core
of the problem?''

To emphasize practical considerations: ''Because you're in an
unusual bind, I'll do my best to get the credit department to give you an extension. But you appreciate
that we can't do this as a matter of regular policy,
don't you?''

How to Cope with the Customer's Questions

What happens when a customer asks questions that are
awkward, aggressive, or unduly inquisitive? At such times you
might prefer not to answer at all or you might fear being tempted
to give a misleading or deceptive answer. The answers of a
salesman who is intent on creating a win-win relationship generally have three characteristics: (1) They will be basically
honest; (2) they will show common sense and good judgment;
and (3) the open, confident manner in which they are given will
help improve the sales relationship.

It is sometimes easy to give completely candid responses to
a customer's tough questions. In other circumstances, a true
but incomplete answer suffices. Or you may be able to beg off
answering at the moment, promising to do so at a specific later
date.

But what about embarrassing questions and those that put
you on the defensive? If the subject matter is peripheral or of
minor significance, it is permissible to try to distract the customer's attention from his question. You can also try to answer
it obliquely. When the question is central to the discussion,
however, you will probably have to face up to it. The manner
in which the answer is given can often save the situation. There
is generally no need to be defensive, tricky, or aggressive. The
answer should be brief, even if that makes it less than satisfactory, so that you can get on to more favorable topics.

How frank should you be? To be totally candid in all situations is naive. Few negotiations can survive complete frankness. Moreover, perfect honesty can sometimes be a disguised

form of hostility. What is required is basic candor so that the customer will not have to wrestle with wondering, "How much of what he's saying can I safely believe?" Here are some guiding questions to ask yourself in difficult situations:

☐ Does the customer have a right to the information he asks for?
☐ Will he use the answer constructively?
☐ Will the answer strengthen the relationship on a long-term basis even though it may temporarily annoy the customer?
☐ How much frankness can the customer bear? Will an honest answer do him more harm than good?
☐ Will the answer help him cope more effectively with his situation?
☐ Is the answer fair to me and my company?
☐ Is the answer one that I can live with without regret?
☐ Is the manner in which I give the answer calculated to improve the customer's respect for me even though he may not like what he hears?

How to Listen with Empathy

Listening is a third skill that can be crucial to successful negotiation. The following pointers may help:

☐ Before listening, try to vacuum your mind of your pet preferences and aversions. Try to listen within your customer's frame of reference.
☐ Listen in an understanding and supportive way. Make sure your attitude is one of empathy—feeling *with* your customer.
☐ Hold your tongue and hear the customer out. Resist the temptation to interrupt, contradict, or argue.
☐ Listen for both meaning and feelings but keep the two separate.
☐ Listen for the "thematic chord" of what the customer is saying. Do not be distracted by incidental remarks or tangential comments.

☐ Do not allow the manner in which an idea is expressed to distract you from its content.

☐ Listen with your whole body. Make eye contact with the customer. Lean toward him. Avoid folding your arms across your chest or tilting your head backward.

☐ Concentrate on what the customer is saying even though it may seem dull or repetitive to you. Remember that you can listen three to five times as fast as he can talk.

☐ Listen to what is not said. Often the real message is contained in what is omitted.

☐ Listen to perceive the shape of the customer's innermost needs so that you can learn to relate to him more effectively.

☐ Don't listen like a mute. Give the customer feedback to show you are with him.

☐ If you must disagree with the customer, never argue. First, restate to his satisfaction what he has already said. Then present your views. Finally, ask for his reaction.

☐ Do not prejudge a customer because of his dress, manners, accent, vocabulary, peculiarities, or other superficial characteristics.

☐ Note but do not react to a customer's attempts to flatter, manipulate, antagonize, or shock you.

☐ "Listen" to what his facial expression, hand gestures, eyes, and body posture are communicating.

☐ Listen in an anticipatory way. Tie in what the customer is now saying with what he is most likely to say subsequently. Attend to the "big picture" and not just to bits and pieces.

☐ As you listen, try to determine why the customer is saying what he says and why he is saying it in the way he has chosen to say it.

Hearing is physiological. When the customer talks, you hear him. But listening is a very taxing psychological task, because it is not natural to be deeply concerned with another person's needs, to stay inside his frame of reference, to think with his brain, to feel with his heart, or to be interested in his gut reactions. It is all the more difficult because you must allow the customer to be master of the situation while you are its servant. He is verbally active whereas you are verbally passive. He is emotionally expressive whereas you must control your feelings. He can say pretty much what he wants in any way he prefers whereas you must be careful how you respond.

It should console you to know that the rewards of listening can be even greater than the difficulties. The cement of any sales relationship is the realization that each negotiator is accepted and understood, that more often than not he can be himself and act naturally, and that each party will be supportive of the other. Listening is the basic binding ingredient of the cement.

How to Motivate Customers

Nothing is more important in negotiation than understanding why customers act as they do and knowing how to motivate them. There is no subject about which so little is known for certain. A list of the important theories of motivation would include these:

Maslow's need-fulfillment theory	Incentive theory
Cognitive dissonance theory	Expectancy theory
Achievement theory	Reward theory
Affiliation theory	Social comparison theory
Competence theory	Self-implementation theory
Herzberg's two-factor theory	Psychoanalytical theory
	Reinforcement theory

The salesman's perplexities are understandable. He will ask himself, Which theory is most applicable? Which theory should I use with which customers? Why do different customers react so differently to the same motives? If psychologists know so much about people, why are there so many theories? How do I know when to stop using one theory and switch to another? What do all these theories have in common, if anything?

There is really no such thing as a theory of motivation. There are many theories, each with its own peculiar assets and limitations. Even though we know that incentives often work, we do not really know why different customers react differently to different incentives.

Even though we know the self-implementation approach to motivation, we do not really know how and why customers differ in their ego strengths. Even though we have been exposed to Herzberg's two-factor theory, we still do not really know why or how the motivational process can be reduced to merely two sets of factors.

In spite of these problems, seven basic guidelines may be suggested to help motivate customers in the negotiation process:

1. Motivation resides in the customer and not in the salesman. Motivation is not what the salesman says or does. It is how the customer reacts.

2. The same motive may provoke different responses from different customers. On the other hand, different motivations may provoke the same reactions from different customers.

3. Since a customer is usually multimotivated, he is trying to satisfy many needs simultaneously according to his own order of priority.

4. To motivate any customer, four competencies are necessary: your ability to read the customer, your skill in practicing motivational techniques, your flexibility in adapting your knowledge to deal individually with every customer, and your realization of what works best for you and what you feel most comfortable with while remaining aware of what is not good for you.

5. You increase your motivational ability not by memorizing long "laundry lists" of human needs but by imitating the scientists. To make progress, they rely on six procedures: painstaking observation; formulation of realistic hypotheses; careful trial-and-error experimentation; sensitivity to feedback to help them adjust their approaches in the light of reactions; discovery of what elicits the most favorable response; and application, using the approach that works best.

6. No salesman can motivate every customer equally.

Sometimes the personal chemistry is wrong between them. By persistence and patience, almost every salesman can nonetheless reach even customers who at first seem totally unresponsive. 7. Motivation is a two-way street. If you accept the challenge to motivate a customer and your goal is to achieve a win-win relationship, then it is wise to allow him to motivate you. When motivation is one-sided, it usually ends up as manipulation.

How to Work with the Motivational Basics

A customer has his own self-concept, ego strength, and level of aspiration

No customer is a motivational blank page on which a salesman can write anything he chooses. As a result of his past successes and failures, the customer has a certain self-esteem. His self-confidence is really self-perceived adequacy. Whereas some customers can take an occasional reversal in stride, others are discouraged at the slightest failure. Some have strong egos while others are weak. One customer may have high expectations and shoot for the moon while another may aim low because his expectations are modest.

Every customer has his own peculiar achievement and affiliation drives

In a sense we are all self-fulfilling prophecies. "Tigers" who have great self-confidence and perceive themselves as winners are success seekers. They fail now and then but their failures merely stimulate them to do better next time. "Turkeys" tend to be failure avoiders. Their fear of failing is a greater motivation than anticipation of success. Customers who are high achievers may not be concerned about what others think of them, but customers who are affiliators and want to be well liked tend to look to people rather than achievement for their need satisfaction.

Every customer has his own unique idea of what is fair

One customer may think that he has been treated equitably as long as the salesman's product works as promised or the after-sale service meets his basic needs. Another customer is always pushing his salesman, making extraordinary demands and requiring special consideration. Unless the salesman takes it as a matter of course, he will find this customer's behavior a pain in the anatomy. If he appreciates that this is simply one of the ways in which customers differ, then, despite his passing annoyance, he can evolve a strategy for coping with him. He can remind the customer that his demands are unrealistic and unfair and that extras cannot be provided as a matter of course unless certain extras are forthcoming from the customer in the form of increased business.

Most customers have a tendency to compare themselves with others

This is known as the social comparison theory of motivation. All success is relative. It is normal for a customer to wonder about whether he is getting the same quantity and quality of service that other customers are receiving and whether the salesman is as interested in him as he is in his other customers. This type of social comparison within a reference group is a basic human trait.

Every customer seeks to satisfy his important needs and wants

Some classifications of human needs are rather brief. Others are quite long. Let's divide them into groups, using their relative importance to sales negotiation as a guide. In the list that follows, the appropriate response of the salesman is given for each kind of customer need.

SURVIVAL AND PAIN-AVOIDANCE NEEDS

Order and consistency   *These are the policies and procedures that I can assure you we will follow to the letter in dealing with you.*

Freedom from surprises and shocks   *Even if we're forced to go to some sort of allocation system, you can be sure you'll get your fair share of our output.*

Avoiding pain and loss   *We pride ourselves on giving the same quality of service to all our customers, big and small. Your interests will not be sacrificed to those of a larger company.*

Safety and security   *We'll see this thing through together. Our people will work with you to guarantee that your results are everything you want them to be.*

Help in time of need   *If you run into any unexpected difficulty, I'll call in our experts to help you out.*

Freedom from fear and anxiety   *I know you're in a tight fix with regard to cash flow, so we'll work something out with our credit department to make it possible for you to pay over a period of time.*

SOCIAL NEEDS

Acceptance, belonging, and conformity   *We've sampled our key accounts and more than 90 percent favor this plan. What do you think?*

Recognition   *Do you mind if I pass this idea along to the home office? It's one of the best I've run across in a long time.*

Interaction   *Why don't we talk it out?*

Approval   *That's a great suggestion.*

Thanks and appreciation   *I want to thank you for being so frank with me in discussing your complaint.*

Participation and contribution   *I'd appreciate whatever input you feel you should make. You've been on your end of the business a long time.*

Friendship and association   *Why don't you sit in on our Sales Executives Club meeting next week? We're having an unusually interesting agenda and there are some people whose thinking I know would benefit you.*

Cooperation *We're in this together. Count on me to do all I can to make it work out well for you.*

Identification *I'm glad we can do business. You're in good company as a major customer of our firm.*

EGO NEEDS

Uniqueness *It's our policy to help you satisfy your specific needs and objectives.*

Independence *My job is to help you decide what's in your own best interests.*

Self-expression *I think we can help you, but first I'd like to get your views on what should be done.*

Privacy and confidentiality *You can be sure that nothing we discuss here will leave the room.*

Self-determination *We've come up with three plans. I'll explain each one and then you can decide which is the right one for you.*

Dominance *Let's try it your way and see how it works.*

Achievement *It worked beautifully. The home office is more than willing to go along with your proposal.*

Growth and development *You may be interested in the dealer development courses our firm sponsors.*

Ego defense *I'm sorry if I offended you. Believe me, it wasn't intentional.*

Self-esteem *Frankly, I think you're one of the sharpest people in the business.*

Status *Before we take any action, I'll consult with you as a matter of course.*

How to Capitalize on Motivation Skills

If you try to be conscious of the following observations, you will be able to avoid the twin traps of being too simplistic and

being too overstructured in your efforts to motivate customers. As with all observations, they do not apply to all customers but do apply to most customers most of the time.
  1. A customer feels motivated when his most important needs are being satisfied. Try to satisfy those needs that are the most significant.
  2. A customer acts logically only to the extent that his needs permit. Don't expect customers to be rational all the time.
  3. A customer has his own unique way of going about meeting his needs. The same need may lead to quite different behavior in different customers.
  4. One customer has the same general needs as all other customers. Discover each customer's priorities among the generalities.
  5. A customer wants a balanced satisfaction of all his needs. Yet he is usually willing to sacrifice needs that he considers less essential in order to meet his high-priority needs. In negotiating, make every effort to see to it that a customer satisfies his central needs since you probably will not be able to satisfy all of them. A customer's needs for security, safety, and social acceptance can be satisfied within the sales relationship.
  6. Each customer differs from all other customers with respect to his self-perceived competence. Help customers in every ethical way to increase their self-perception of capability.
  7. A customer has a specific mind-set at the beginning of his initial negotiations with you. This is the result of his past successes and failures in dealing with salesmen. Learn what his mind-set is. If it is negative, you may have to work to change it before you can start negotiating with him.
  8. A customer is tempted by risk and fearful of failure. Help customers take on acceptable risk while minimizing the paralyzing effects of fear. Every customer will be somewhere on the continuum of success seeker and failure avoider. Find out just where your customer stands and adapt your negotiation strategy to fit his situation.
  9. A customer has his own specific goals and level of aspiration. Direct your efforts toward helping him reach his goals. Success is not measured only objectively. It is also a subjective

feeling that the result was better than the customer's level of aspiration allowed him to anticipate.

10. A customer deals with you because he expects to obtain desired benefits. Learn what his expectations are and help him fulfill them.

11. A customer expends certain nonmonetary costs in time and energy when he works with you. He expects to receive a certain return on his investment. Provide him with the rewards he is looking for.

12. A customer has social affiliation needs. Help satisfy them by offering a close, consultative type of relationship within which the two of you can create a partnership.

13. A customer wants to increase his pleasure as much as possible and minimize his pain. If you must say or do anything distasteful, make certain that it is counterbalanced by compensating satisfactions.

14. A customer seeks reinforcement. Go out of your way to give him positive support whenever it is justified.

These directions for capitalizing on your motivational skills can be summarized in a simple formula:

$$\text{Satisfied customer} = \frac{\text{rewards perceived}}{\text{investments} + \text{costs}}$$

The rewards a customer receives are defined by him, not by you. Investments represent the experience and expertise that the customer channels into the negotiation process with you. Costs include the time and effort he spends with you. These are the expenses of interacting that make up his contributions to the sales relationship. If you use negotiation to maximize a customer's rewards, there will be little need to worry about motivating him.

Sales negotiation is essentially a form of *social exchange*. Whenever a customer feels he is getting more out of his exchange with you than he is investing in it, he will be motivated not only to continue the relationship but to seek more of it.

4

How to Acquire the
Knowledge Base for Negotiation

You will require three kinds of knowledge for successful negotiation: insight into your customer organizations, understanding of your customer decision makers, and self-awareness.

How to Understand Your Customer's Organization

Pope John XXIII once remarked to a visitor, "Even as the Pope, I cannot really do what I want." Every customer operates with constraints. Every decision maker reacts to certain fields of force. He is a focus of disparate likes and dislikes and conflicting preferences and aversions. He is also a spokesman for a complex network of power, authority, and status. These constraints and power sources may remain a mystery to a salesman who has not learned how to map his customer's organization accurately and weave his way through the corporate maze.

Any company, division, or department with which you do business is a sausage-link series of interacting systems, each of which induces its own particular behavior pattern. Figure 7 shows some of the more prevalent types of systems and their principal patterns of customer behavior.

To the novice salesman, a customer company may appear calm and placid. The experienced salesman knows better: the

Figure 7. Organization systems and customer behavior.

Types of Systems	*Principal Behavior Patterns*
The authority system, where some people have great clout and others have little	Most people are jealous of the power they have while trying to add to it
The power system, where people have different kinds and amounts of power	Most people strive to augment the kind and amount of power they have
The political system, where the art of the possible is carried on	Some people jockey and elbow each other for positions of prominence
The status system, where privileges and prerogatives are distributed unequally	Some people maneuver to add to the trappings of their office
The influence system, where only some people have access to the ear of the powerful	People try to influence key officials as much as possible
The technical system, where people are organized in units to achieve company goals	People collaborate within units but also work at cross purposes as individuals
The social system, where organization goals and personal aspirations blend	People use the organization to attain personal objectives
The organizational system, where the organizers manage the organized	People set up informal organizations outside the establishment to meet their own needs
The motivation system, where management strives to energize subordinates	People work to satisfy their own motives
The reward/punishment system, where some people are richly rewarded and others are passed over or penalized	Individuals try to secure as many organizational "goodies" as possible

company's policy statements, operating procedures and rules, position descriptions, organization charts, and accountability statements are all geared to tasks, not people. In them, "skim milk masquerades as cream." The salesman must pierce the polite facade, the impersonal etiquette, and the dignified decorum that characterize a customer's paper organization and must get at the true organization. It is people who get things done in an organization and, at the same time, create most of the salesman's problems.

The "people" organization in a customer company—the "real" organization—is a microcosm of life in general. Side by side are friendships and hostilities, high hopes and wrecked ambitions, teamwork and selfish egoism, temporary coalitions and lasting alliances, ingroups and outgroups, collaboration and conflict, winners on a fast track and losers who have been derailed, leaders and followers: the best and the worst in human nature working shoulder to shoulder.

What does all this imply? It means that the salesman must first ask the right questions regarding his customer's organization and then arrive at answers that are reasonably accurate. Figures 8 and 9 show a method of self-questioning designed to bring out an organization's style and operating characteristics.

A salesman can also ask himself other questions: Are the key decision makers failure avoiders? Success seekers? Maintenance caretakers? Tradition and habit-bound conservers? Improvers and innovators? Management-by-objective advocates? Cooperative and team-oriented? Additionally, it will help if the salesman is.tuned in to the company's traditions, philosophy, taboos, and mores—the important codes of corporate behavior that never appear in print.

How to Understand Your Customer Decision Makers

Identifying the real buyer is at times quite difficult. This is especially true in large, complex, customer organizations. The real buyer is the decision maker who can give business to you or withhold it from you. He may or may not be the individual

Figure 8. Organization style characteristics.

Leadership Style		
Democratic	Autocratically centralized	Bureaucratically departmentalized
Paternal	Exploitive — dog-eat-dog	Laissez-faire, loose leadership

Human Relations Style		
Mutually supportive	Competitive	Formal and politely proper
Friendly and relaxed	Politically exploitive	Mutually aggressive

Communication Style		
Free, open, and direct	Informal and sporadic	Primarily grapevine
Formal channels only	Secretive among ingroups	Imperious from top down

Decision-Making Style		
Autocratic, by one man	Autocratic, by one group or function	Consultative
Negotiated and accommodative	Democratic participation	Local, functional, and decentralized

Figure 9. Organization operating characteristics.

Tempo		
Brisk and fast-paced	Impulsive and erratic	Tail-chasing and wheel-spinning
Crisis-centered and fire-fighting	Deliberate and progressive according to plan	Slowmoving and ultracautious

Self-Image		
Industry leader — "We're No. 1"	Runner-up — "We're No. 2"	Young comer
High-growth company	Industry innovator	Mature industry statesman

Value Orientation		
Bottom-line profit orientation	Technology orientation	Product orientation
Market and customer service orientation	Tight-ship, low-cost orientation	Risk-free, survival orientation

Personality		
Energetic and opportunistic	Lethargic and ponderous	Sensitive and suspicious
Conflicted and divisive	Confused and perplexed	Nervous and uncertain

you call on. At other times, he may be merely an influencer or a recommender rather than a decision maker. Decision making is a process of applied power. A decision maker is in a position to impose his will and make himself felt. Power is a heady feeling. All decision makers are energized by it. They find it one of the most positive aspects of making decisions. Several other positive characteristics flow from power. Authority is one of them. The decision maker has authority because he must be considered. You cannot ignore him and go around or over him. This gives him importance. It confers status on him.

Power gives a decision maker influence over salesmen. He can affect you, your results, and your emotions. This gives him a certain amount of control over you and all other salesmen who negotiate with him. Not only does he affect their destinies, but he also influences the destinies of people inside his own organization; and by virtue of the purchase decisions he makes, he reacts on his company's customers as well. This gives the decision makers a greater or lesser sense of responsibility for their decisions. They feel depended on by others. There is a need for them. If it is true that we all need to be needed, decision makers are always aware of the need for the role they play.

These positive attributes of the decision-making process are almost universal truths. They are the desirable accompaniments of decision-making authority that make it coveted. But other, downside attributes of making decisions often conflict with the pluses, sometimes diminish their pleasure, and occasionally nullify their rewards.

When a decision maker accepts power, he trades off some types of security and comfort. Decision makers always confront risk. They anticipate being wrong and worry about what will happen if the decisions they make turn out to be wrong. Decision makers are also apprehensive about being blamed. Blame is the other side of being responsible. For many decision makers, the buck stops with them.

Uncertainty surrounds many of the most common buying decisions. What if there is really something better? What if there is something cheaper? What if there is something that is both better and cheaper? Is there a joker somewhere in the deal? Am I being snookered? Uncertainty about the outcome of decisions creates loneliness in many decision makers. They feel isolated and abandoned. Organizationally and politically, they can turn to no one to share in their deliberations or in the disapproval and disrepute that may result from them. Many salesmen take advantage of this situation to get close to customer decision makers by offering them consultative companionship.

These negative features of making decisions frequently make decision makers reluctant to use their power to decide. They may prefer to postpone decisions rather than make them now. Because experience tells them that problems often solve themselves, they usually hope that many really sticky situations will disappear that way. Even the pressure of making relatively minor decisions over and over again may cause reluctance to make one more or resentment over having to do so. To a harried decision maker, the world can seem filled with ''decisions, decisions, decisions.''

These positive and negative generalizations about what it is like to be a decision maker are a useful background for reading each individual decision maker before you negotiate with him. It is safe to assume that the generalizations probably apply. What you must determine is exactly which of them apply to the greatest degree. Then, within this overall context, you will have a helpful guide to the specific reading of each decision maker that will clue you in to the best mix of negotiation strategies to use with him.

Once you have pinpointed the real buyer, you need some idea of how he goes about reaching a decision and of the positive or negative roles he finds most comfortable. Figure 10 can serve as a guide in recording your impressions.

In addition to learning what roles your customer decision maker plays with you, it is also important to know his needs. In this context, the word ''needs'' refers to a decision maker's expectations of salesmen, the roles he hopes they will play with him, and the ways in which he anticipates that salesmen will

Figure 10. Basis, time frame, and mode for decision making.

1	Basis for Decision Making			2	Time Frame for Decision Making			3	Mode for Decision Making	
	Rational		Sensory							Shares decision making with these *influencers:*
	Facts only	Facts and concepts	Gut feeling only	Facts and feeling		Short term	Deliberate	Prolonged		Solo	
											Name/title: ___
											Name/title: ___

Positive Roles Played by Decision Maker

4									
Guide and adviser who helps me plan my strategy	Information source who gives me access to facts	Supportive "friend at court" who goes to bat for me	Problem formulator who clues me in to the real problems	Problem-solving partner who helps me reach solutions	Helpful devil's advocate who prepares me for possible resistance	Incisive questioner and answer seeker	Fair and equitable judge who mediates internal conflicts for me	Door opener who introduces me to new opportunities	Permissive yea-sayer who gives me free access

Negative Roles Played by Decision Maker

5									
Petty fault-finder who nitpicks	Aggressive confronter who challenges me at every turn	Forceful and vigorous dominator of my plans and actions	Agile game player who counterploys and counterploys with me	Shrewd politician who connives for every advantage over me	Dishonest manipulator of my inputs when he conveys them to others	Deliberate delayer who uses time as a bargaining tool with me	Highly personal and nonobjective interpreter of my work	Constant pleader for special privilege from me	Highly introverted withdrawer from me

relate to him. Figure 11 will help you organize your knowledge of a decision maker's needs.

How Influencers Can Affect Your Decision Makers

Since no decision maker is an island, you must know the people who influence him. This involves knowing not only the kinds of pressure they can bring to bear on his buying decisions but also the source of their power. Furthermore, you should be familiar with the various roles that influencers are likely to play, both positively and negatively. Figure 12 provides a format for doing this.

If you can make friends with a real buyer's influencers, your task can be made easier. On the other hand, they can shoot you down if you work at cross purposes with them. Accordingly, it is prudent to search out the expectations of these influencers, the ways in which they want salesmen to relate to them, and the needs they have of them. Figure 13 enables you to do this.

Figure 11. Decision maker negotiation-needs profile.

Wants to be well liked: needs me as a friend	Prefers to be respected rather than liked: needs me as an admirer	Is a young man on the way up: needs my savvy and guidance	Is a stickler for detail: needs plenty of documentation, verification, and reassurance from me	Is a gossip collector: needs me to bring him tidbits	Is neck and neck for the top spot: needs me to help him win a big one
Is paternal: needs to make me his client and help me	Is a born teacher: needs me to be his star pupil	Is weak in an important trait or discipline: needs me to be his counselor	Is isolated with no one to talk to or confide in: needs me as a confidant	Is on shaky ground politically: needs me as a nonvoting supporter	Is almost over the hill but still has power: needs me to honor him

© The Greenhouse Group, Inc., "The Greenhouse Group Decisionmaker Analyzer." Reproduction is expressly prohibited.

Figure 12. Types and basis of influence.

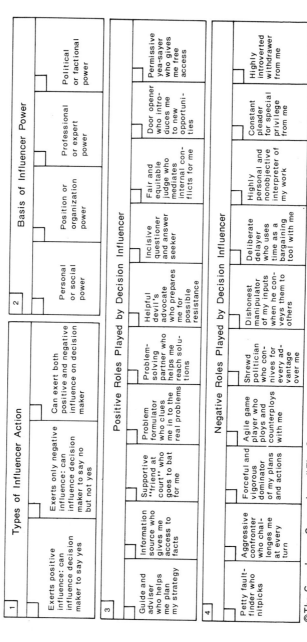

	Types of Influencer Action		
1			
Exerts positive influence: can influence decision maker to say yes	Exerts only negative influence: can influence decision maker to say no but not yes	Can exert both positive and negative influence on decision maker	

	Basis of Influencer Power		
2			
Personal or social power	Position or organization power	Professional or expert power	Political or factional power

	Positive Roles Played by Decision Influencer			
3				
Information source who gives me access to facts	Supportive "friend at court" who goes to bat for me	Problem formulator who clues me in to the real problems	Problem-solving partner who helps me reach solutions	Helpful devil's advocate who prepares me for possible resistance
Guide and adviser who helps me plan my strategy				
Incisive questioner and answer seeker	Fair and equitable judge who mediates internal conflicts for me	Door opener who introduces me to new opportunities	Permissive yea-sayer who gives me free access	

	Negative Roles Played by Decision Influencer			
4				
Aggressive confronter who challenges me at every turn	Forceful and vigorous dominator of my plans and actions	Agile game player who connives and counterploys with me	Shrewd politician who connives for every advantage over me	Dishonest manipulator of my inputs when he conveys them to others
Petty fault-finder who nitpicks				
Deliberate delayer who uses time as a bargaining tool with me	Highly personal and nonobjective interpreter of my work	Constant pleader for special privilege from me	Highly introverted withdrawer from me	

When you have used it to analyze each major influencer, it can be very helpful to compare the roles and needs profiles of your real buyer and his influencers.

How Groups Can Affect Your Decision Makers

As companies become more complex, the basic unit of reference is the group and not the individual. It is the work group, not the individual, that gets things done. Psychologically, too, the group is important. Customers are social beings as well as professionals. They are intensely interested in what their reference groups—that is, the groups with which they identify—think of them. This makes it important for you to know about group dynamics and the effects that groups can have on their individual members who may be your decision makers or their influencers.

Figure 13. Decision maker influencer-needs profile.

Wants to be well liked: needs me as a friend	Prefers to be respected rather than liked: needs me as an admirer	Is a young man on the way up: needs my savvy and guidance	Is a stickler for detail: needs plenty of documentation, verification, and reassurance from me	Is a gossip collector: needs me to bring him tidbits	Is neck and neck for the top spot: needs me to help him win a big one

Is paternal: needs to make me his client and help me	Is a born teacher: needs me to be his star pupil	Is weak in an important trait or discipline: needs me to be his counsellor	Is isolated, with no one to talk to or confide in: needs me as a confidant	Is on shaky ground politically: needs me as a nonvoting supporter	Is almost over the hill but still has power: needs me to honor him

©The Greenhouse Group, Inc., "The Greenhouse Group Decisionmaker Analyzer." Reproduction is expressly prohibited.

What is a group?

A group is two or more individuals who have a well-defined objective in relating closely and continuingly to one another.

What kinds of groups are there?

There are all kinds of groups: formal and informal, cohesive and conflicted, task and social, collaborative and competitive, and interacting and counteracting.

What needs does a cohesive group meet?

☐ It provides social satisfactions and support for its members while defining what is real and significant for them.

☐ It makes it easier for members to interact and influence one another.

☐ It can be a powerful agent in altering the attitudes and behavior of its members, because each group has its own reward-punishment system and its own standards of acceptable behavior.

☐ It makes it easier for members to take risks that would be unacceptable to them as individuals.

☐ It makes it easier for members to deal with fear and anxiety. In unity there is confidence.

☐ It pressures individuals to conform to its expectations.

☐ It provides support for ideas and actions that its individual members would normally not espouse without the backing of the group.

☐ Members of the group tend to act on the values of the group as if they were their own.

☐ It exerts social controls over the behavior of the members.

☐ It protects the members from attacks by outsiders.

☐ It influences each member to think of himself in terms of how the group evaluates him, especially if he is other-directed in personality.

☐ It is an efficient communications medium.

The group is in a position to help its members satisfy many basic needs: acceptance, security, pride, status, identity, aggression, communication, teamwork, and reinforcement.

How effective are group approaches to problem solving and decision making?

☐ Group discussion is often far more effective in changing individual attitudes than one-on-one methods are.

☐ Groups are often very effective in analyzing a situation and coming up with realistic recommendations because many points of view are considered.

☐ Group support can help decisions be accepted and implemented.

☐ Cohesive groups work harder and more persistently than groups that are not so cohesive.

☐ Cohesive groups stimulate their members to accept individual responsibility for the outcome.

☐ Groups often end up with a less than desirable decision or solution because of the need to achieve consensus.

☐ A group often comes up with a decision that is more mediocre than its best individual member would arrive at but it is usually a more acceptable and more workable solution.

☐ Even without trying to, groups tend to enforce "groupthink" and behavioral conformity.

☐ Groups can be quite resistant to change, and many groups have a built-in restriction on innovation and creativity.

☐ Groups often overemphasize togetherness to the neglect of individual initiative and task achievement.

☐ At times, a group will protect its own provincial interests at the expense of the overall good.

It is evident that a group is a two-edged sword. It is therefore necessary that you know what kind of groups you are dealing with, how each group interacts and responds to other important groups, and what strategies you will use in coping with the key groups that pressure your decision makers. Figure 14 will help you answer questions of this sort.

Every customer is the representative of his organization. More importantly, he is a unique individual in his own right, intent on meeting his own needs and wants. We have previously referred to the denominator of the "human fraction": the

Figure 14. Group influence profile.

The _____ Group
(Name of apparent leader)

☐ Ingroup currently   ☐ Up-and-coming   ☐ Outgroup wielding
   wielding power   group striving   negative power
                           for power

Cooperation/Competition Relationships

1. This group *cooperates* with
    1. The _____ group.
    2. The _____ group.
    3. The _____ group.

2. This group *competes* with
    1. The _____ group.
    2. The _____ group.
    3. The _____ group.

Sales Decision Influence

This group makes sales decisions.	This group influences individuals or other groups that make decisions.	This group provides decision-making information as a resource group.
This group has a vested interest in delaying or defeating sales decisions.	This group can nullify the practical effect of a sales decision by withholding its cooperation.	This group implements sales decisions after they have been made.

© The Greenhouse Group, Inc., "The Greenhouse Group Decisionmaker Analyzer." Reproduction is expressly prohibited.

commonalities shared by everybody. We will now zero in on the numerator, the individual differences that make each buyer unique.

How Individual Differences Can Affect Your Decision Makers

In negotiating, every salesman must be prepared to contend with several different types of decision makers:

The rational buyer, who is primarily concerned with what is logical in a salesman's presentation

The irrational buyer, who acts rationally only to the extent that his biases permit

The knowing buyer, who desires to learn as much as he can from a salesman

The seeking buyer, who wants to acquire and retain all the values available to him

The social buyer, who aims to be well liked

The emotional buyer, whose nerve endings may blot out his cognitive processes

The idealistic buyer, who is likely to do the best he can to live up to his ideal self-concept

Understanding intellectual style

A customer's intellectual style consists of six factors: speed of comprehension; intellectual preference; mental capacity; cognitive orientation; typical intellectual pace; and ability to think, judge, and reason. Figure 15 provides a guide for synthesizing these factors, which are summed up in psychological terms as *cognitive style.*

Understanding psychological style

As a spokesman for his organization's interests, a customer decision maker is rightfully concerned about its objectives. In every negotiation, he must necessarily have an eye to what's in it for him as an organization man as well as what he will get out of it that is personally satisfying. The psychological needs he hopes to fulfill in the negotiation process constitute his personal agenda. Figure 16 can help you become sensitive to a decision maker's psychological pattern.

Understanding personality style

Personality is the trickiest concept in customer psychology. It can be defined as the characteristic that enables you to predict how the customer is likely to act in given situations. Figure 17 presents a format you can use to see beneath the mask that

Figure 15. Analysis of decision maker's intellectual pattern.

	ABOVE AVERAGE	AVERAGE	BELOW AVERAGE
Speed of Comprehension (Select one)			
Wax-wax: Quick to learn, quick to forget	———	———	———
Wax-marble: Quick to learn, slow to forget	———	———	———
Marble-marble: Slow to learn, slow to forget	———	———	———
Marble-wax: Slow to learn, quick to forget	———	———	———
Intellectual Preference (Rate all)			
Abstractions: Prefers ideas and theories	———	———	———
Concrete situations: Prefers practical problems	———	———	———
Social situations: Prefers to deal with people	———	———	———
Cognitive Complexity (Select one)			
Simplistic: Black-white, either-or type of thinking	———	———	———
Orderly: Logical and concise	———	———	———
Complex: Delves deeply into ramifications	———	———	———
Cognitive Orientation (Rate all)			
Language: Comfortable with words	———	———	———
Numbers: Comfortable with numbers	———	———	———

Figure 15. *(Continued)*

People: Comfortable with people	———	———	———
Ideas: Comfortable with theories and abstractions	———	———	———

Cognitive Movement
(Select as applicable)

Slow and plodding: A patient thinker	———	———	———
Fast-paced: A rapid thinker	———	———	———
Unconventional: Has far-out ideas	———	———	———
Conservative: Cautious thinker	———	———	———
Imaginative: Creative and innovative thinker	———	———	———
Thoughtful and reflective: A deep thinker	———	———	———

Evaluative Capacity

Ability to size up situations	———	———	———

every negotiator wears. Several cautions, however, are in order:

- [ ] Customers are synergistic. Every decision maker is more than the mere sum of his personality traits.
- [ ] Personality characteristics, especially in the course of a negotiation, may change from time to time and from situation to situation.
- [ ] It is the clustering of a customer's personality attributes that is significant, not simply their presence or absence.
- [ ] The same traits may be expressed in different kinds of behavior. One decision maker may be aggressive because it is "natural" for him. Another may be aggressive because he is overcompensating for what he perceives as a tendency on his part to be too easygoing.

Figure 16. Analysis of decision maker's psychological pattern.

He has a need for: (Rate as applicable)	HIGH	AVERAGE	LOW
Power			
Dominance over others			
Affilitation			
Control of situations			
Achievement			
Attention			
Increased competence			
Ego-building responses			
Aggression			
Deference to others			
Status and prestige			
Independence			
Recognition			
Sense of adequacy			
Sense of self-esteem			
Dependence			
Success orientation			
Failure avoidance			
Risk taking			
Closeness with others			
Social distance from others			
Hostility			
Interaction with others			

☐ A decision maker's characteristics are often responses to his salesman's behavior.

☐ It is easy for a salesman to perceive a decision maker's more obvious attributes but fail to note those that are less flamboyant but no less significant.

Understanding value systems

The most important attributes of a customer are his values. A value connotes at least four things: It is a conviction concerning what should be done or left undone; it is a standard for judging behavior; it is a criterion for determining the relative worth of situations and people; and it is a guide for behavior. The following values can be found in almost every customer decision maker:

Political values   He may be conservative, liberal, or middle of the road.

Economic values   He may be an adherent of unlimited free enterprise, an advocate of business-government cooperation, or a defender of capitalism-with-a-conscience.

Social values   He may feel either that government should ignore social problems or that it should legislate social solutions or intervene actively in their solution.

Aesthetic values   He may be unconcerned with culture or he may be quite concerned about the fine arts.

Philosophical values   He may be interested only in the mundane and the practical or he may be sensitive to philosophical questions and issues.

Ethical values   He may have primitive ethics or he may be convinced that moral knowledge must be matched with moral courage.

Every salesman must come to appreciate that whenever he attacks a customer's value system he assaults the nucleus of the customer's personality, regardless of where the truth may lie or what the salesman may think. For this reason you must constantly keep your personal radar sweeping throughout

Figure 17. Analysis of decision maker's personality traits.

He is inclined to be (Rate as applicable)	1	2	3	4	5	
Open and authentic	—	—	—	—	—	Secretive
Emotionally mature	—	—	—	—	—	Lacking in self-control
Self-sufficient	—	—	—	—	—	Dependent
Cooperative	—	—	—	—	—	Exploitive
Self-objective	—	—	—	—	—	Self-deceptive
Cautious	—	—	—	—	—	Venturesome
Considerate	—	—	—	—	—	Self-centered
Conservative	—	—	—	—	—	Liberal
Friendly	—	—	—	—	—	Antagonistic
Energetic	—	—	—	—	—	Passive
Even-tempered	—	—	—	—	—	Moody and changeable
Gregarious	—	—	—	—	—	Introverted
Conventional	—	—	—	—	—	Unconventional
Self-assured	—	—	—	—	—	Timid
Predictable	—	—	—	—	—	Erratic
Positive-minded	—	—	—	—	—	Negative
Cooperative	—	—	—	—	—	Aggressive
Independent-minded	—	—	—	—	—	Conforming
Future-oriented	—	—	—	—	—	Past-oriented
Spontaneous	—	—	—	—	—	Reserved
Inner-directed	—	—	—	—	—	Other-directed

every negotiation to pick up any early-warning signals that you are offending your decision maker's most basic convictions. Much the same advice applies to gaining insight into a customer's assumptions, prejudices, and aversions. Freud once remarked that, when he started his career, he felt it would be impossible to understand another human being. With experience, he found the job was not nearly so difficult because his patients were always telling him about themselves when describing their behavior. If you have your antenna up and tuned in to your customers, you will find it increasingly easy to sense the assumptions on which every customer is operating, his likes and dislikes, his biases and prime interests.

How to Understand Yourself

Up to now we have been examining how you can understand your customer. What about the other side of the coin? While you are trying to understand a customer, he is also involved in trying to perceive you accurately, even though his responsibility for understanding is much less than yours. The third component of the knowledge base you need for negotiation is therefore your own self-awareness. Because our good intentions so often blind us, no one is easier to misperceive or to fool than ourselves. Since self-knowledge is the beginning of wisdom, you will be well advised to give some thought to your own role in the give-and-take of negotiation.

An effective way to analyze yourself is to use the same instruments that help you understand your customers. Over and above this self-diagnosis of your decision-making style, the roles you prefer to play in negotiation, and your individual differences, you can gain additional insights into yourself by your answers to these questions:

☐ What are my attitudes toward customers in general? Why do I have such attitudes? To what extent do they help or hinder my efforts to negotiate with them?

- [ ] What assumptions underlie my interaction with customers? Are they the correct assumptions regarding myself, my customers, and our negotiations?
- [ ] What are my strengths in relating to customers? How can I capitalize on them more fully?
- [ ] What are my remediable limitations? What strategies can I formulate to correct these deficiencies?
- [ ] What are my unchangeable defects? What are my strategies for living with them without permitting them to lessen my effectiveness?
- [ ] When I enter a negotiation, what is my self-image? How do I perceive my role? Are these self-perceptions reasonably accurate or do they hurt my efforts to negotiate?
- [ ] What are my expectations of a customer in a negotiation with me? Are these expectations realistic?
- [ ] What are my prejudices and stereotypes about customers that lead me to prejudge them without evidence? What can I do to counteract my prejudices lest they undo my efforts to negotiate?
- [ ] Where am I vulnerable psychologically? What are my pet peeves and my sacred cows? What strategies can I use to prevent these highly charged responses from worsening the negotiation process?
- [ ] Where am I vulnerable emotionally? What are the areas where a customer's ego-inflating behavior makes me a willing victim of emotional seduction?
- [ ] What is there about my usual ways of interacting with customers that alienates them or prompts them to raise their defenses? How can I convert these patterns into other actions that are more likely to build win-win relationships?
- [ ] What do I like about myself? What don't I like about myself? Are these likes and dislikes based on reality or on self-deception?
- [ ] What do customers generally like about me? What do they tend to dislike? What can I do to maximize what they like and minimize what they dislike?
- [ ] How compatible are the things I like about myself with

those that customers generally like about me? How can I increase this compatibility?

☐ To what extent, and for what reasons, do I generally win the respect of clients? What prompts them to lessen their respect for me?

☐ What kind of climate do I create in my dealings with customers? What can I do to improve it?

☐ What is my reputation with customers? What can I do to make it even more positive?

☐ When my customers talk about me with their associates, what would I most like them to say? Why? How can I increase the probability that they will say it? What would I least like them to say? Why? What can I do to reduce the probability of their saying it?

☐ What satisfactions am I really seeking from my negotiations with clients? Why do I need these particular satisfactions? Are they the right ones for building lasting relationships?

The more self-understanding you have, the greater the insight you are likely to have into your customers. After all, *to the other fellow you are the other fellow.* Your own self-insight makes it easier for every one of your customers to negotiate with you in a true one-to-one relationship.

part two

Creating the Essential Relationship

5
How to Partner
Your Customers

The basic approach of cooperative negotiation is to make your customer an ally, not an adversary. The whole idea of negotiation is based on finding areas of agreement on which you and a customer can make common cause. The major area of agreement to seek out is mutual profit improvement: You improve the customer's profit by helping him apply your products and services in ways that will cut his costs or increase his sales revenues; in return, the customer helps you improve your own profit contribution on sales by paying you a premium price.

Two people whose relationship with each other is built around mutual profit improvement are *partners*. Only partners can maximize the values of negotiation.

The "We" Approach to Partnering

The essential ingredient of all partnerships is always the same. It is simply that two can improve profit better than one. By working closely together with your customer as a team, you can create a cooperative "we" orientation for your relationship instead of a sometimes rivalrous, often aggressive-defensive "me-you" orientation. As "we," you can supplement and complement each other in achieving objectives of a higher order, reinforce each other's capabilities, invite third and fourth parties onto the team when they can make a necessary contribution, and fend off problems and problem makers who pose a common threat.

Partnerships are built by experiencing good works together. Being partners is generally the result of accomplishment over time. More accurately, it is the result of multiple accomplishments over considerable time. While it is occasionally possible to become instant partners with a customer by being cooperative with him in a single crisis situation that you successfully see through together, most partnerships are the result of passing many tests under a wide range of circumstances. Persistent performance is the keynote.

Common Denominators of Partnering

Being a partner is one half of a sales relationship. Converting a customer into a partner is the necessary other half. All partnering is based on four common denominators:

1. Partners have *common objectives*. Each partner wants to improve his pride and profit.
2. Partners have agreed on *common strategies* for achieving their objectives. Their methods are initially based on mutual need seeking and then on mutual need fulfillment arrived at through cooperative negotiation.
3. Partners are at *common risk*. Each partner has something of equal value, or at least significant value, to gain or lose.
4. Partners have a *common defense* against all others who are not included in the partnership. Each party deals with his partner as an equal. Outsiders range from being less equal to being perceived as competitors.

Cooperative negotiation strategies enable partners to treat each other as equals. This is the principal rule of partnership. There are ten additional rules that can serve to guide you in selecting and applying your cooperative strategies. These are shown in Figure 18.

The basic business of partnering is two parties doing valuable things for each other. What's more, they *keep doing* valuable things for each other. If one partner stops contributing to the enterprise, the partnership stops. A partnership can therefore be summed up at any time as an energy system whose net worth is the total value of the things currently being done in it.

Mutually Rewarding Partnering

Three valuable things are going on all the time in a mutually rewarding partnership between a salesman and his customer.

Figure 18. Rules of partnership.

---

1. Add value to each other. Teach each other new ways to improve personal actualization and professional productivity so that both partners profit by the relationship.
2. Be supportive of each other, not competitive. Form a staunch team.
3. Avoid surprises. Plan your work together and work according to your plan.
4. Be open and above board. Level with each other by telling it like it is.
5. Enter into each other's frame of reference. Learn each other's perceptions so that you can see things from the other's point of view. Learn each other's assumptions so that each of you can understand the other's expectations of the partnership.
6. Be dependable. This means being reliable. Partners must be there for each other when they are needed.
7. Anticipate opportunities and capitalize on them. Anticipate problems and steer the partnership around them. Keep the partnership out of trouble. If trouble is unavoidable, give the partnership a head start in solving it.
8. Do your homework. Know what's happening in the area of the partnership's operations so you can make a professional contribution to its activities.
9. Treat each other as people, not just as functionaries. Be willing to provide the personal "little extras" that make a partnership humane as well as a mighty force.
10. Enjoy the relationship and make it enjoyable to your partner. Both of you should prefer to work within the partnership rather than any other relationship because it is one of the most rewarding associations either of you has ever had.

First of all, the partners are sharing in improved profit. The second major benefit that partners confer on each other is the shared experience of learning together just how their profits can be improved. A partnership should be a breeding ground for generating new knowledge of profit making and putting it to work with shared faith and shared apprehension. The act of learning together is one of the strongest bonding agents in a customer-salesman partnership. It is the growth element in the relationship because it ensures that both partners will grow.

The third attribute of a successful partnership is mutual support. Each partner divides the relationship's labor according to his individual capabilities. The complementary nature of the relationship enhances each of them. Contrariwise, each partner is diminished by the absence of the other.

These three benefits—accomplishing shared objectives, learning together, and supporting each other—are the cornerstones of customer-salesman partnerships. Other benefits accrue around them. The partners can help their relationship by motivating each other when the going gets tough, keeping each other honest, and playing the outfield for each other so that outsiders will find it hard to score points against the partners.

From a salesman's point of view, being a partner in a mutual profit-improvement relationship can be translated in this way: "My products and services, plus my personal expertise in applying them, can help my customers improve their profit. They may help cut customer costs or help earn new sales revenues. As a result, I can improve my own profit contribution because I can sell more, or sell more often, or justify a premium price for what I sell."

In the act of partnering a customer, three areas of needs must be brought into harmony:

1. *Mutual need revelation,* which allows you and your customer to understand honestly what each of you wants out of a deal.
2. *Mutual need adjustment,* which helps you and your cus-

tomer to give where you can give while you both hold fast where you cannot yield.
3. *Mutual need fulfillment,* which means that you and your customer are both winners.

Through a partnership approach, profit becomes the bulls eye objective that you and your customers share in common. Negotiation is the language partners use with each other as each strives to improve the partnership's profitability.

Consultant/Client Partnering

To make a partnership work, one more thing is necessary. The salesman must be positioned as a consultant and the customer must be positioned as his client. A consultative salesman has three distinguishing characteristics. First, he sells the profit improvement benefits of his products and services rather than the products and services themselves. Second, his major stock in trade is his mix of personal expertise and customer information that allows him to apply his products and services to cut customer costs and improve customer sales revenues. And third, he has converted his customers into clients.

The customer conversion process is the focal point in positioning yourself as a consultant. It is absolutely essential because a consultant cannot consult with a customer. The thrust of a customer will always be to position a salesman as an optional supplier of a product or service whose major difference from competitive offerings is its lower price. A consultant, on the other hand, can command a premium price because he has branded his products and services with the added value of his applications knowledge.

A customer can be converted into a client only by repositioning his traditional role. Repositioning requires recognizing what may be called his "perfect rights of clienthood." If you grant a customer these rights and make it clear to him that you recognize that he now possesses them, you can manage his conversion. There are six principal rights that every client can expect from his consultant:

1. Improve my profit—quantify your contribution.
2. Talk my language—understand my business.
3. Be a bargain—give me value that is superior to your price.
4. Be professional—give me cost-effective solutions.
5. Teach me—share your knowledge with me.
6. Be available—give me access to you when I need you.

A consultative salesman and a product salesman are two different animals. The product salesman tells his customer *what* he has to sell. He is product proud. He tries to get his customer to tell him how his product can be applied. "What uses do you have for a product like mine?" is his favorite question. The consultative salesman tries to get his client to ask him *how* an important business problem can be solved or *how* an opportunity can be seized in a way that improves profit. When his client asks him how, the consultative salesman tells him what effects his products and services can have in improving client profits. Then, as partners, they negotiate a sale.

part three

Choosing and Using
Your Strategy

6

How to Sort Out
the Issues for Negotiation

Reading yourself is an exercise in self-perception. Reading your customer decision makers and their organizations is an exercise in translating their various communications about their needs, wants, and desires into meaningful clues about how to negotiate with them. When you have completed these two homework drills, you are ready for the second discipline: sorting out the issues to be negotiated.

Sorting is a process of refinement. Almost all situations involving a customer's complaints, requests, or innovations that either he or you have introduced into the relationship require refinement. Typically, you will find that the areas of agreement that always accompany the areas of controversy can be considerable. Sometimes the areas of agreement plus the areas about which neither of you cares very much will add up to as much as 90 percent of an entire issue. The remaining 10 percent will be the stickler.

That sticky area will contain the differences you will have to *define* and then *refine* before you begin to negotiate. Refining the issues makes negotiation possible. Otherwise you and your customer might bargain interminably about what seems to be the issue rather than what the issue really is. Refining the issues also makes successful negotiation probable. The narrower the problem and the fewer the number of issues that the problem can be reduced to, the greater probability that you and your customer will both win your negotiations.

A simple schedule of two sorting steps can help you segregate the issues worth negotiating from their surrounding areas of agreement and indifference. The first step is to define the areas of difference. The second step is to refine them into "essentials" and "expendables" so that the expendables can be negotiated. Figure 19 shows an Issue Sort Schedule based on this sequence.

Figure 19. Issue sort schedule.

Define the areas of difference . . .

If your customer complains to you, makes requests of you, or introduces an innovation with you,
1. Have him state his proposal.
2. State your response.
3. Define the differences to your mutual satisfaction.

If you introduce an innovation to your customer,
1. State your proposal.
2. Have your customer state his response.
3. Define the differences to your mutual satisfaction.

Refine the areas of difference . . .

Group the issues in the areas of difference into two classifications:
1. The *essentials,* which are the core issues that neither you nor your customer can give up. Reduce the number of these essentials to the bare minimum to give you maximum room to maneuver in negotiation.
2. The *expendables,* which are the issues that are susceptible to negotiation.

Negotiate the expendables . . .

Choose and use the optimal mix of negotiation strategies so that both you and your customer come out as winners of your mutual objectives.

Define the Areas of Difference

A negotiable situation can arise from your own initiative or as a result of any one of three initiatives that a customer may take with you.

If Your Customer Takes the Initiative

Your customer may come at you with a complaint, seeking to use it to gain leverage against you for a concession of some sort. Or he may request that you sweeten a deal or provide free services over and above what you normally offer. A third initiative he may take is to introduce an innovation in your relationship by making a change in buying policies or practices, specifications, self-manufacture, or competitive relationships that can adversely affect your participation in his business.

In any of these situations, you can begin to define the areas of difference between you and your customer by first asking him to state his proposal. When he does, and if you understand it, then state your response. The two of you should then be able to define the differences between his proposal and your response in a way that can meet with your mutual satisfaction.

If You Take the Initiative

If you come at your customer with an innovation in your relationship that he may be initially uncomfortable with or may be unpleasantly surprised by, you can begin to define the areas of difference by first stating your proposal from his point of view. This means that you present the benefits to him before you hit him with the bad news. If you must present a price hike, for example, first introduce any compensatory benefits he will derive so that the value-to-price relationship he perceives in his dealings with you will still be overbalanced on the side of value. If your innovation is to introduce another salesman to the account as a partial supplement to or an eventual replacement for you, first provide reassurance of your continued availability and control. If you do this part of your presentation well, you can significantly reduce or perhaps eliminate altogether the areas of difference between you.

After making your proposal, have your customer state his response. Ask probing questions to smoke out his full reaction. Then, when both of you have put all your cards on the table, define with him any remaining areas of difference between you.

Refine the Areas of Difference

Once the areas of difference between you and your customer have been brought to the surface, the next step is to refine them into two classifications. The first classification is the "essentials." These are the core issues that neither you nor your customer can afford to give up. Essentials are usually personal or professional conventions that may be thought of as ethics, precedents, traditions, or eternal truths. You should try to reduce the number of essentials on both sides to a bare minimum. The more numerous they are, the greater constraints they impose on your room to maneuver in negotiation because essentials are essentially nonnegotiable.

When the essentials have been minimized, you can turn your attention to the "expendables." These remaining areas of difference between you and your customer are the issues that are susceptible to negotiation.

7
How to Choose and Use
Your Negotiation Strategy

When you have completed your prenegotiation homework—
which means that you have read yourself, your customer decision maker, his influencers, and his organization and then
sorted out the issues for negotiation by the defining and refining
process—you are ready to choose and use your negotiation
strategy mix.

Your choice of negotiation strategies will be structured,
either wholly or in part, by the type of sales situation in which
you find yourself with a customer. Some situations give you a
broad choice of strategies. This is especially true of cooperative situations where you and your customer have clearly
mutual objectives you want to achieve and your bargaining
power is more or less equal. In other situations, you may be
forced to take a defensive position before you can turn the
situation around into a cooperative one. Your range of choice
in strategy selection will therefore be much more limited.

There is a third type of situation. Occasionally, you and a
customer will be headed for genuine conflict with each other.
Cooperative negotiation will be impossible. Even your defensive strategies may not work in restoring the situation. You will
then have to choose a resolution strategy that will enable you to
avoid conflict or allow you to confront it in a negotiable
manner.

In Chapter 8 you can learn how to choose and use *coopera-*

tive negotiation strategies. Chapter 9 discusses *defensive* negotiation strategies. *Conflict resolution* strategies are spelled out in Chapter 10.

How to Make the Three Basic Estimates

Most negotiating situations are made up of a few facts and many assumptions. Some assumptions are so universally borne out by experience that you can almost accept them as facts. You can assume with a high degree of confidence that to be a customer in a negotiating situation is to be a worried man. A customer is always apprehensive about being wrong or making a mistake. Suppose he's blamed for his decision. Suppose his decision doesn't work out. Suppose he's overruled because there was something better, cheaper, or both that he could have agreed to. Suppose he's called on to justify his decision. All these anxious anticipations can haunt customers when they negotiate with you. They make customers uncertain, hesitant, and reluctant to commit themselves.

Against this common background, choosing the best negotiation strategy for each situation is an exercise in making three estimates. If you make them properly—in other words, if your assumptions are accurate—your strategy selection will narrow itself rather quickly to a range of usable approaches that should include the single strategy or strategy mix you can use with confidence. The three estimates are *evaluation of your customer's needs in the situation, evaluation of your own strength,* and *a careful evaluation of your downside risk.*

In many negotiation situations you will have access to some hard facts that will help you firm up your evaluations. In other situations you will have only hearsay, rumor, third-party subjective judgments, and a random assortment of clues ranging from body language to explicit statements of attitude or opinion. The great majority of situations include a blend of fact and fiction. Even more confusing, alleged facts may turn out to be fiction. In the final analysis, the only wise way is to make your own estimates out of all the information at hand plus your own knowledge and intuition.

Estimate Your Customer's Needs

There are two aspects of your customer's needs that you should evaluate to help determine your choice of negotiation strategy. One is to make an assumption of the type of needs that your customer has on the line. Are they solely professional? Or are they reinforced by personal needs as well? It is rare that these two types of needs remain separate and distinct. Almost all professional business situations are intermixed with personal needs like achievement and self-expression. These personal needs complicate business situations. In a tough negotiation they sometimes become more important than the business problems that may appear on the surface to be the only problems being bargained.

If you estimate that only a business problem pure and simple is involved, a single negotiation strategy may suffice. If your customer has a personal involvement in the outcome—not just in winning the negotiation but also in the continuing events that will follow—you may have to mix two or more strategies. You may need to select a cooperative strategy for the business bargaining and a defensive strategy for the personal involvements, or the other way around.

The second important aspect of customer needs that you must evaluate is their degree of intensity. In the customer's opinion, how strongly are his personal and professional needs involved in the negotiation? To the extent that he is strongly committed, he will be a tougher bargainer. You may have to prepare yourself to trade off more than you would otherwise plan to yield or take a firmer stand earlier in your negotiation.

Use Figure 20 as a model to write out your estimate of your customer's needs and their degree of intensity in advance of every major negotiation.

Estimate Your Own Strength

No matter how well you know him or how long you have done business together, it is always difficult to make an accurate assessment of a customer's needs or their strength. But it may be even more difficult to estimate your own strength going into a negotiation. We usually overestimate ourselves. This can be a serious mistake. If you overestimate your own strength and at the same time underestimate the strength of your customer's needs or position, your compounded error can be fatal to a win-win negotiation.

To avoid overinflating the amount of leverage you believe yourself to have in a negotiation, you should make a conservative estimate of the strength you bring to it. Are you in the right

Figure 20. Estimate of customer needs.

Customer Name: _____

Statement of problem or opportunity in impending negotiation:

_____

_____

Personal Needs	*Degree of Intensity*		
1. _____	High	Medium	Low
2. _____	High	Medium	Low
3. _____	High	Medium	Low
4. _____	High	Medium	Low
5. _____	High	Medium	Low
Professional Needs			
1. _____	High	Medium	Low
2. _____	High	Medium	Low
3. _____	High	Medium	Low
4. _____	High	Medium	Low
5. _____	High	Medium	Low

from a factual point of view? Can you prove it? If you succeed in proving it, can you win the negotiation but lose the relationship? Is your position weak? If so, how can you strengthen it or defend yourself strongly as a means of weakening your customer's position? These are some of the questions you should ask yourself before each negotiation. Use Figure 21 as a model

Figure 21. *Estimate of my own strength.*

In negotiation with (customer name):_____

Statement of problem or opportunity in impending negotiation:

_____

_____

_____

Elements of Strength in My Position	*Degree of Intensity*		
1. ———————————	High	Medium	Low
2. ———————————	High	Medium	Low
3. ———————————	High	Medium	Low
4. ———————————	High	Medium	Low
5. ———————————	High	Medium	Low

Elements of Weakness in My Position			
1. ———————————	High	Medium	Low
2. ———————————	High	Medium	Low
3. ———————————	High	Medium	Low
4. ———————————	High	Medium	Low
5. ———————————	High	Medium	Low

Net Estimate of My Resulting Leverage	High	Medium	Low

to write out your estimate of your own strength in advance of every major negotiation.

If you are going to make a mistake in either direction, it is safer not to give yourself the benefit of any doubts you may have about your leverage. It is easier to revise your estimates upward in the course of a negotiation, after being pleasantly surprised, than to have to revise them downward. There is no sense in fooling yourself when you will not be able to fool your customer.

Estimate Your Downside Risk

As you prepare yourself for a negotiation, try not to get so wrapped up in contemplating what you can win that you forget to calculate what you can lose. Ask yourself, "What is the

Figure 22. Estimate of my downside risk.

In negotiation with (customer name): _____

Statement of problem or opportunity in implementing negotiation:

_____

_____

_____

Estimate of What I Can Lose	*Probability of Loss*		
1. ———————————	High	Medium	Low
2. ———————————	High	Medium	Low
3. ———————————	High	Medium	Low
4. ———————————	High	Medium	Low
5. ———————————	High	Medium	Low
Net Estimate of My Downside Risk	High	Medium	Low

most I can lose in this negotiation?'' This will give you insight into its degree of importance to you. If you have little to lose, your downside risk is small. You can afford to be generous. On the other hand, if your downside risk is large, you must choose and use your strategy mix with great care. In advance of every major negotiation, use Figure 22 as a model to write out your estimate of your downside risk.

8
How to Use Cooperative Negotiation Strategies

Cooperative strategies are the basic tools of negotiation. Their purpose is to create and then maintain win-win relationships with your customers. Cooperative strategies are mutually supportive. They pose no threat to either negotiator, allowing both you and a customer to deal with each other from positions of strength and self-respect.

The end result of practicing cooperative negotiation strategies is to "partner" a customer, that is, to make him your partner in improving the profit of both his business and your business. You improve his profit by helping him reduce some of his costs or earn new sales revenues through using the products and services you sell. You improve the contribution to your own company's profit by selling him more of your products and services or by selling more of them at a premium price that is justified by their ability to reduce his costs or earn new sales revenues for him.

Partnership is the key to mutually profitable sales relationships. It is therefore the objective of all negotiations with your customers. Cooperative strategies begin to build partnership. Defensive strategies can help you preserve partnership under stressful circumstances and restore it when it becomes imperiled. Your partnership will inevitably need to be defended from time to time. But for the most part, you should strive to protect your partnerships from becoming defensive by practicing cooperative negotiation in every sales situation.

When you adopt cooperation as your central partnering strategy, you abandon the traditional competitive approach to your customers. You no longer attempt to win sales at their expense, put them into a defensive posture with you, take short-term advantage of their needs at the cost of the longer-term values of the relationship, or regard them as adversaries whose objections are things to be overcome rather than understood and who are to be "closed" whether they are ready to be or not. Cooperative negotiation will set you apart from other salesmen who practice percussive persuasion. It will also help distinguish your offering by adding to it the value of teaching profit improvement to your customer. This approach can help isolate you from competitive sales propositions that may otherwise be identical to your own and can help consolidate your position as the preferred supplier.

Cooperative Strategies and How to Use Them

All cooperative negotiation strategies have a common denominator: They are based on the principle of teaching. Their purpose is to teach the facts of a situation or to teach how to get them and apply them. Shared knowledge of the facts is the firmest foundation for cooperation. Without the sharing, continuing dissent and disagreement on "what the facts are" will disrupt any partnership and ultimately lead to a divorce. With agreement on a common body of facts, especially when accumulation has been a shared experience, partners can plan together and take joint action to achieve mutually improved profits.

To help you teach your customer how to work with you in your common interest, you should learn how to use five cooperative negotiation strategies:

1. *Trial balloon*, which will enable you to make proposals to your customer without committing either of you, without creating defensive reactions, and with the best chance of teaching him and learning from him at the same time.

2. *Devil's advocate,* which will enable you to launch trial balloons for teaching and learning purposes only, not for action.

3. *Look at the record,* which will enable you to refer to a current, accurate fact base as the true source of your proposals and thereby depersonalize customer negotiations.

4. *Trade off,* which will enable you to set up a give-and-receive cycle with your customer in which you both teach and learn, gain and yield.

5. *Small bite,* which will enable you to add value to your customer's business on a successive achievement-by-achievement basis whose price is affordable and whose encompassable size does not challenge his believability or disorganize his operations.

Trial Balloon

If there is a single distinguishing characteristic that is shared by successful sales negotiators, it is that they are all professional trial balloonists. They make their give-and-take suggestions largely in the form of trial alternatives that they inflate with a mix of facts taken from the record and that they float across the reactions of their partners.

Every trial balloon has the same first name, "What if." By prefacing each suggestion or recommendation by a "What if," you can defuse any implicit or overt threat of dominating the partnership by becoming its major influence or by taking an excessively aggressive role. By phrasing your proposals in the form of questions, you present the customer with options whose acceptance and implementation you are telling him you would like to negotiate. You make it easy for him to accept it because you are giving him the right of first refusal. You make it easy for him to enter into a dialog with you so you can teach him why his answer to your proposal should be a yes.

Before you can receive acceptance of a "What if," you must get your customer's permission to teach him the benefits of acceptance in relation to the investment he will have to make to obtain the benefits. The response that enables you to begin *teaching*—which is the negotiator's word for *selling*—is the customer's return question, "How?" Cooperative negotiation is the act of exchanging "What if" and "How" questions back and forth between the negotiators.

Trial ballooning helps you avoid the need to take a stand that could commit you to a point of view too early in a negotiation. This keeps you from having to defend an unpopular proposition or from being regarded by your partner as exploitive or manipulative instead of cooperative. It also keeps down the pressure on your customer to make an unfounded decision, either positive or negative, before he has the facts, or it keeps from predisposing him to reject a proposal because he fails to understand its initial thrust.

The third word in every "What if" proposal is the partnering word "we." The cooperative preface to your negotiations that asks, "What if we . . . ?" invites a customer to respond with the selling invitation, "How can we?" Or he can respond with a counterproposal that is also prefaced by his own "What if." In this way, trial ballooning can stimulate each negotiator's second and even third efforts to come up with the best possible proposal within the context of a mutually beneficial friendly rivalry.

Model Scenario of Trial Ballooning

SALESMAN: This is a stickler, all right, but let's see what we can do to work our way around it. [Emphasizing the "we" approach to being partners.] What if we try to improve profit by controlling inventory costs more tightly? [Launching a trial balloon.]

CUSTOMER: I'd like to stay off that area right now—let's say for organizational reasons.

SALESMAN: All right. [Demonstrating second effort.] What if we try to improve profit by directing our cost-cutting attention to the distribution process—specifically, to your trucking operations that require backhauling? Suppose we could improve profit by 5 to 7 percent.

CUSTOMER: I thought we'd squeezed out most of our distribution costs already. How would you go about making new savings?

Devil's Advocate

A devil's advocate type of trial balloon is launched in order to teach something to a customer or to learn something from him, but not to have him take you up on it. It is a "What if?" that does not expect a "How?" in return. Instead, it is designed to elicit, a "Why?"—"Why would you want to do anything like that?"—or a "What?"—"What would the purpose of something like that be?" In some cases, a flat "No" from the customer followed by your own question, "Why?" will be the purpose of the devil's advocate balloon.

A devil's advocate balloon can be used to teach a customer something you have in mind to propose to him in the future. The time is not ripe yet. But it is a good time to get him thinking ahead, rehearsing your recommendation in his mind, and gradually becoming comfortable with it. He will probably shoot down the balloon today. Nevertheless, he will be more familiar with its message the next time he sees it. This, of course, will be when you float it seriously as a regular trial balloon.

The second reason to float a devil's advocate balloon is to learn something from a customer about how he sees his business, where his innovative or experimental boundaries are, how far the political climate inside his company will let him go, or what information sources he may be acting on or lack.

Devil's advocate ballooning is a form of trade-off. Every time you lose a balloon by customer veto, try to learn why. For every balloon you lose, come back with a trade-off balloon whose name is "If we can't do that, *What if* we do this?"

Sometimes there is a value in "flying high" with a devil's advocate balloon. By flying in high, either in the grand scope of your proposal or its price, you leave room to scale down voluntarily as soon as you have floated the balloon and before your customer can react. This is a straw balloon. You will shoot it down yourself but not before the customer has experienced the strength of your total capabilities, for instance, or perceived the maximum range of your value-to-price thinking.

Model Scenario of Devil's Advocating

SALESMAN: [Floating a devil's advocate balloon.] What if we were to create a master list of cost reduction opportunities that you and I, working together, can affect—and to do it, what if we could get together with the managers of manufacturing, engineering, sales, and R&D?

CUSTOMER: [Shooting down the balloon.] How would you and I ever get a group like that together? From their point of view, why would they come?

SALESMAN: [Floating a different balloon.] You're raising a good point. What if we begin to think about how we can put on an educational program for them that will upgrade their understanding of our objectives?

Look at the Record

Partnerships are paradoxical. They are emotionally charged alliances, commanding a good deal of strong, positive feeling by both partners about the values they derive from their relationship. Yet along with their emotional charge, partnerships depend on agreement about what constitutes the facts the partners will use as the foundation for their negotiation.

Facts supply the partnership with the key component of honesty. They ground the relation in the real world, lend it the substance rather than the mere semblance of truth, and rule out the destructive practice of endlessly bickering over who is right and who is wrong. Because it is the partnership that must be right, both partners have a theoretically equal responsibility to maintain its base of recorded fact. In practice, however, you should be prepared to accept the lion's share of the burden.

Cooperative negotiation is very largely dependent on looking at the record over and over again. One of the founding acts of partnership should be construction of the team's data bank, an easily accessible repository of current, accurate facts about two central subjects. The first is how the customer makes his profit, which requires knowledge of why his heavy-user customers buy from him, why they continue to buy more, and how they perceive the benefits of his big-winner products or services. The second is knowing the constraints against the customer's profit-making capability, which requires knowledge of the location and contribution of the customer's cost centers and the contribution made to them by his need to cope with competition; legislative constraints that affect his products, marketing, pricing, employment practices, and environmental responsibility; ups and downs in the economy; market trends in population growth, purchase preferences, and use of discretionary income; and technological innovation.

These are the facts that should be used as the platform for the sales-growth plan that you ought to prepare with every key customer. They are also the facts to which you and your customers can refer to avoid or settle disputes about the situations in the economy or in the marketplace that you are trying to affect. By seeking recourse to the record, you and your customers can jointly participate in a learning experience in which both of you can simultaneously witness the discovery of evidence and obtain reassuring guidance from authoritative sources. Shared learning experiences such as these are the most powerful factors in creating partnerships.

When you go to the record you are using facts and figures as testimonials that in effect are silent third-party conciliators. Facts on the way are the cooperative negotiator's equivalent of "Here come the marines!" They can save the day for you and your partnerships by acting as a shield against any competitive salesman who would like to de-partner you by teaching your customer a different view of the real world: that salesman's view.

If you have to defend your right to negotiate because your customer perceives your offer or your credibility as being weak, you may have to present overwhelming factual evidence that you deserve consideration. Insofar as possible, your evidence should come from an expert external source that your customer recognizes as authoritative. If you do not know which sources he credits, ask him. Your own company's internal staff people are generally a less desirable option since they can be suspected of bias. If you are forced to rely on them, back them up as much as possible with third-party expertise. Any time you say to a customer, "Let's look at the record," remember that facts and figures do not negotiate. Salesmen and customers do. No matter how incontestable evidence may be, it cannot guarantee that you will be invited to negotiate based on it. Evidence must be presented so that a customer can perceive how he can benefit from its implications. You must therefore be its interpreter and applier, not simply its collector and presenter. While you should always strive to make your evidence 100 percent correct, as much as 80 percent of its effectiveness in giving you the leverage you require to negotiate can come from the way you present it.

If you lean on facts as your platform, be sure they are facts. Document their validity, both for your own protection before you present them and for your customer's reassurance afterward. He may have to defend them inside his own organization. You should therefore give him all the help you can so he can act as your agent. If your facts turn out to be fiction, both of you will be hurt. His wounds may be critical. Yours will probably be fatal.

Model Scenario of Looking at the Record

SALESMAN: With the updated cost figures you've contributed to it, our proposal now seems to be extremely well geared to taking advantage of the new product opportunity we sense in the marketplace.

CUSTOMER: I agree that there's probably opportunity out there. But just how much and for how long, I don't know.

SALESMAN: Let's go back, then, and look at the facts once more and see if they can help us arrive at a level of confidence we can act on. [Using the record.] The market opportunity data have been corrected to reflect the recent government constraints against the ingredients used by your competitors, as well as changes we can expect in

market development costs due to current inflation rates.
Let's see what we can learn.

Trade Off

Cooperative relinquishment of one aspect of a proposal in
exchange for accepting a customer's equivalent, substitute, or
replacement is the essence of negotiable give and take. Such
trades should be made voluntarily, without pressure, to incorporate the customer's contributions into your proposals so that
they can become "our" proposals. It is less *giving up* than
gaining. This qualification distinguishes cooperative trading off
from defensive trading off, which is more in the nature of a
concession that must be made rather than an advantage that
can be gained.

Trade-offs occur naturally in the course of cooperative
negotiation when both you and a customer use the "What if"
approach. Instead of accepting your "What if" in its entirety,
the customer may barter with a "What if" of his own. You can
then integrate his suggestion into your proposal or counter with
your own revised "What if." This sort of reciprocal exchange
can take place several times, each exchange fleshing out the
original proposal, adding new or more relevant dimensions to
it, and engaging the participation of the negotiating partners in
ever-increasing depth.

The ongoing information exchange that tit-for-tat trade-offs
provide should be the principal teaching and learning medium
for the partners. Each can transmit his own sense of what is
most appropriate and needs doing first, making priorities
known in an informal manner that does not incur the risk of
talking down to the other party by pontification or lecturing.

A willingness to trade alternatives and the ability to be a
constructive trader, building on the strengths of every option
and trying to eliminate its weaknesses or irrelevancies, are the
central ingredients required to make negotiation a workable
dialog. They are also the central qualities of creative negotiation, since they act as the spark plug for new ideas and for
producing exciting insights that would otherwise go undiscov-

ered. When partners look forward to negotiating with each other because it revitalizes them and helps them grow professionally as well as in their interpersonal relationships, they are anticipating the next installment of their reward for trading off cooperatively.

Well-managed trades make a virtue of second effort. The difference between a highly productive partnership and mediocrity is often determined by the motivation of each partner to make a consistent second effort to trade for better alternatives. This is not meant to suggest that negotiation is an unending game of "Can you top this?" However, it does emphasize the added value of hanging in, of doing your homework so that you can ensure a rich flow of ideas, and of educating your customers in the actively suggestive role you want them to play with you.

Model Scenario of Trading Off

SALESMAN: What if we go to work to improve your package graphics as a strategy to improve profit by obtaining new sales?

CUSTOMER: We might be able to use some help there, but not much. Our in-house people do a pretty good job on graphics. They must. We keep winning awards.

SALESMAN: Well, let's not intrude on something that's functioning at a high level of performance. [Trading off by demonstrating second effort.] What if we turn our attention to new product development? Our market research people have some excellent new information on emerging needs in your customer's industry that could be the basis for new sales revenues.

CUSTOMER: How about discussing graphics in the context of the new-product-development opportunity?

Small Bites

Many negotiable situations must be managed in an evolutionary manner. This means that you should think small at the beginning and proceed by taking successive small bites of a customer's business on a slice-by-slice schedule. Taking small bites is a modular strategy, building a climate of confidence and a track record on a gradual basis. The net result of this sausage-link approach can be significant business.

Small bites allow a partnership to emerge out of mutually rewarding experiences. This strategy is practically free of pressure, except the pressure to perform. The burden is on every individual sales proposal to achieve its objectives. A single failure can be fatal. No reservoir of faith exists to draw from at the outset, or for some time thereafter, if things go wrong. For this reason, every miniproposal that is to be negotiated should have minimal objectives. Above all, they should be achievable within a relatively short time frame. This says that evolutionary partnerships should adhere to the golden rule of EVR: early visible results.

Every gradualistic proposal you make is a form of sampling. You allow a timid or reluctant customer to test-market your offering in a way that saves him from having to make a major commitment up front. Since his risk is always small, he will have little to lose while he tests whether or not to invest a more substantial portion of his trust with you. Nor will he have long to wait to find out if his investment will pay off or if he will have to call a diplomatic halt to the evolutionary process if he cannot perceive results.

When you set about to make a series of trial offers, the major downside risk you face is the possibility of opening and closing in one presentation. A second risk is that your cost per miniproposal may be high in comparison with its limited return. A third risk is that you will not be able to achieve truly significant objectives with small-budget, short-time-frame proposals even though they meet the criterion of providing early visible results.

In proposing a test case to start an evolutionary chain, it is best to make two things clear to your customer. The first is that the trial is part of a complete program of several interlocked proposals whose total cumulative effect you will spell out. The second is that the trial can also be considered as an entity in itself, with its own meaningful objectives and rationale. This type of presentation can embolden your customer to accept the test case, since he can visualize it as a separate project that can stand on its own merits with no strings attached. It can also help predispose him to accept a second miniproposal and then the entire program as it fully evolves.

When you begin to sense that your customer is growing comfortable with your relationship, you may want to combine two or more of your planned miniature proposals into a more formidable presentation. This is accelerated gradualism. In Darwinian terms, the small proposals that you absorb all at once into a larger proposition will become missing links. External factors such as a transient market opportunity, a threat of competitive action, a technological jump, or an opportune event in the business cycle are all good reasons to consider accelerating the chance to take leadership or head off a problem. Special occasions like these allow you to depart from the precedent of gradual evolution and introduce an innovative pace and style into your partnership.

Model Scenario of Biting Small

SALESMAN: Just in the past several months, a growing number of high technology businesses in several fields have implemented the system we've just examined. [Looking at the record.] With only a few exceptions, we started with a small first step to make sure of our footing. [Emphasizing the small-bite approach.] Then, when we felt we were on firm ground, we kept taking additional small steps toward our eventual objective.

CUSTOMER: Did you have all the steps planned out in advance or did you put each one together when you felt it was ready to go?

SALESMAN: All in advance, just as we'll do with the opportunity you have. The plan will spell out every step and relate it to every other step. We'll build them as modular units. That way, we can evaluate any module's individual contribution and make sure it pays off with measurable early results.

CUSTOMER: Suppose a module doesn't work out or the whole system idea seems about to bomb out. Can we cut our loss quickly and get out?

SALESMAN: Usually within 90 days. Let's see what the first trial step would look like.

Foot in the Door

A small bite approach can be effectively used to get a foot in a new customer's door. There are two principal factors to bear in mind when you use this strategy. One is the nature of the foot you choose. The other is what you do with it once you get it in the customer's door.

A trial offer can be the foot in the door. You can offer to give your customer a trial slice of the loaf by proposing a small initial order and making the rest of the order contingent upon his experience with the first slice. Think small. Suggest that he try one of something, that he try something once, or that he take advantage of this once-in-a-lifetime offer. The words "one" and "once" can be door openers. To emphasize the conditional nature of your offer, encase it in a tight time frame. Emphasize early visible results by providing a cutoff time by which the customer's trial will be rewarded. If the cutoff time cannot be short, provide cutout points along the way so the customer can stop his loss if satisfactory results are not forthcoming.

Once your foot is in the door, you must be successful. Second chances are rare when you ask for just one opportunity. If you succeed, you have a choice of two tactics:

1. *Wiggle your toes.* You can take the gradual approach and continue to make haste slowly. Continue your successful strategy by proposing a series of small individual steps, each with its own cutoff time or with cutouts along the way. You can maintain this strategy indefinitely or wiggle your toes faster once your customer has gained confidence.

2. *Kick in the door.* You can adopt a strategy of escalation and follow up your trial offer with a full-scale proposal designed to go all the way or at least a good part of the way. If

you get to the halfway point through a gradual approach, you can make a bid for completing the job by suggesting that the customer can't stop now because he's almost there. Keep in mind that if you try to kick in the door too soon, you may find yourself on the outside once again, this time perhaps to stay.

Model Scenario of Biting Small to Get a Foot in the Door

CUSTOMER: We already have second sources all across the board. Other than in an emergency or on an unusually good price basis, I don't see our using you in the immediate future.

SALESMAN: [Putting his foot in the door.] Once you have firsthand experience of the operating advantages we can deliver, you'll move us up as a source. What if we help you in one of your toughest problem situations? We'll study it carefully and tell you in dollars and cents what you can expect within the first 90 days.

CUSTOMER: Well, let me think it over for a while. Maybe we can work something out.

SALESMAN: [Trading off.] We'll set it up for you with 30-day cutouts so you can cancel without obligation before the 90-day trial expires.

CUSTOMER: Would you be prepared to follow through if everything worked out in the trial so we wouldn't lose headway?

9
How to Use Defensive Negotiation Strategies

Customer partnerships are dynamic. They are always changing, very often in ways that you cannot control or even influence. For example, you cannot control policy changes that take place inside a customer's business which put new pressures on him by restructuring purchasing policies or performance standards. You cannot control demand changes that take place in a customer's market that affect his sales and marketing strategies, his product construction or composition, or his pricing. What you cannot control, you must anticipate. And what you must anticipate is that you can suddenly be made to go on the defensive at any time in your partnerships.

There are three main causes of the defensive negotiation situations in which you will find yourself. One is *customer complaints*. Another is *customer requests*. Complaints and requests cannot be ignored. They must be attended to either by defensively acknowledging them or defensively resisting their effect on your contribution to the partnership. In any event, since they possess the power to restructure the relationship in your customer's favor, they carry with them the threat of ending the partnership.

Outright failure to perform on your part can cause a complaint. Heroic remedial measures on your part can cause a request for similar performance all the time. But you can be performing in a perfectly acceptable manner and still suddenly be made defensive by an *innovation* in your partnership. This is the third main cause of defensiveness. The facts of the customer's business may change. His objectives may change. His attitudes, which are known as "corporate policies" when they are formalized, may change. Perhaps most difficult of all to cope with, his loyalty may split off from you to another partner. Your relationship may become a triangle and the threat of the third partner may force you to become defensive.

How to Close the Door on the "Third Partner"

To the four basic characteristics distinguishing a partnership—common objectives, common strategies for achieving them, common risk, and common defense—a fifth can be added, common sharing of knowledge. This is the best strategy for shutting out third partners.

In essence, every partnership is an information transfer machine with an endlessly repetitive two-phase cycle: teach-learn, teach-learn, teach-learn. Each partner teaches the other, and each partner learns from the other. In this way, information moves back and forth, transferring knowledge so that the expertise and experience of each partner becomes the common property of both.

A partnership's information transfer machine is the generator of its growth. Without the ability to grow, partnerships die. Some partnerships grow slowly. Others experience rapid growth. As the partners grow, they grow closer because they are growing together. If one partner begins to grow faster than the other, he may outgrow the partnership.

A growth relationship where new learning is always going on, where the partners are learning *about* each other as well as *from* each other, presents an almost impregnable situation to anyone who seeks to repartner one of its members. What added value can a third party promise?

A competitive salesman who would like to repartner your customer has a formidable task if you are managing your partnership's information transfer machine in a professional manner. To do this, you must transfer to your customer the type of information that can help him learn how to improve his profits. In return, your customer must transfer to you the type of information that can help you learn how his profits can be improved, namely, where his costs cluster so that you can reduce them and why his customers buy from him so that you can help him earn new sales revenues. This leaves a competitor with two options.

He can try to repartner your customer—or, to say the same thing in another way, to departner you—by outbidding you on the degree to which you claim you can improve customer profit. If you are promising profit improvements of 3 to 5 percent, let's say, he may promise to teach your customer how to achieve improvements of 7 to 9 percent, or even more. Anything less adds insignificant new value and is not worth considering.

This type of competitive approach has two problems. First, it may lack credibility. Your customer may reject it out of hand as unrealistic. It will almost certainly create discomfort if not disbelief. Second, it will require your customer to consult with you about how such a promise could be made, let alone achieved. This will give you the opportunity to share your knowledge with him and, by the very act of exploring the problem together, you can bring the partnership back into harmony.

The other option open to a competitor is the familiar one of departnering you by underbidding. The competitive salesman may promise to make the same or a greater improvement in customer profit as you do but for less. Remember, though, that anytime more is offered for less, it challenges credibility. Here, again, an opportunity is created for reinforcing the partnership by consultative information transfer. You must bear in mind, however, that a competitive salesman who can charge less and truly improve customer profit as much as you do, or more, has earned the right to be your customer's new partner.

Your role in managing your partnership's information transfer machine vis-à-vis competition can be summarized simply. You must develop the customer's profit so well that you force competition to become *incredible when they try to outbid you on performance* or to become *unprofitable when they try to underbid you on price*. This is the best offense you can maintain. And in negotiation strategy making, the best offense is the best defense. But because there will always be times when you must go on the defensive, you should know the basic defensive negotiation strategies and how to use them.

Defensive Strategies and How to Use Them

All defensive negotiation strategies have a common denominator. They are based on the principle of defusing a disputed or potentially disruptive situation and buying time to establish a new fact base that will enable the partners to deal with the situation reasonably. A defensive situation signals you that you need a new fact base. Because you may be unprepared, your primary need will be to create some "learning room" before you negotiate a solution so that, once again, you can restore the essential basis of cooperative negotiation by teaching your partner the facts and how to apply them.

To give you time to establish a new fact base, you should learn how to use five defensive negotiation strategies:

1. *Fall back*, which will enable you to retreat to previously prepared positions on a step by step basis and to take a stand if you need to at the point when your win-win relationship threatens to become win-lose for you.

2. *Trade off*, which will enable you to barter concessions on your part for customer concessions.

3. *Turnaround*, which will enable you to reposition a complaining or requesting customer, renovate his argument, or react first to steal his thunder.

4. *Call for help*, which will enable you to introduce into the situation an authoritative third party who represents a new fact base or an objective endorsement of the existing one.

5. *Take a walk*, which will enable you to cool off a hot dispute, put time and space distance between you and a customer, and come back later with the facts.

Fall Back

Every negotiation carries with it the possibility that you will have to fall back and defend yourself in depth. You should therefore always enter a serious negotiation with a plan that calls for you to retreat to a previously prepared position on a step-by-step basis. The back-steps you take should begin with the most minor concessions you can think of. Each back-step should represent a progressively more important consideration. Ultimately, your final fallback will be the position where you must take a stand.

Your first step back may not require that you surrender anything of substance at all. Sometimes just indicating a willingness to negotiate further will be acceptable as the first step back. From that point on, you can choose among three tactics:

1. *The half-step.* You can offer to yield a position without actually yielding it. The best device to use is a contingent offer. It only half commits you because it is dependent on approval by higher authority in your company. By attaching a provisional string to your fallback, you make it conditional on forces beyond your control. When you go up the line for approval, you buy time. You also create suspense. If you choose to deliver on your hedge, the suspense can end in a feeling of relief that may far transcend the actual value of the benefit you have yielded. In effect, you will have provided added value through relief of tension. Even if the customer's suspense ends in disappointment, you may still appear heroic by virtue of having tried. Because you have extended yourself, you may be credited with making a concession even though you have sacrificed nothing.

2. *The one-step.* You can give way one step at a time, bargaining harder each time you leave one position for another. The harder you bargain, the more time you can buy and the more opportunity you allow for the play of other factors that can distract or divert your customer's concentration.

3. *The two-step.* After retreating to one or two of your previously prepared positions, you can unexpectedly offer up your next two fallback concessions as a unit. This may appear to be magnanimous on your part, encouraging the customer to accept. It may also appear to be your final offer. This can hasten acceptance by itself.

When you can anticipate the need to fall back, try to calculate in advance just how deep a defense you will need. This will help you set a pace for your defense. An important factor to consider is the frustration tolerance of your customer. Some customers enjoy prolonged negotiation. Others are so frustrated by it that they may respond with ill will toward you for putting them through the wringer even though they win in the negotiation. Every now and then you will find a customer who prefers to reduce his frustration by breaking off the negotiation. If this happens, you will have to decide whether he is genuinely acting out his frustration or using the negotiating strategy of breaking off discussion by taking a walk.

A defense in depth must be a defense with honor. Whatever points or positions you concede must be surrenderable without damaging the benefits you can deliver to your customer when the negotiation has been completed. Otherwise you cannot concede them. You must not try to wangle back anything you have given up. Nor can you retain the privilege of complaining ex post facto or of attributing the customer's failure to receive full benefits from your eventual proposal to what he forced you to give away. If you cannot afford to give away a position, you should not offer it.

As you execute your fallback, avoid the temptation to bluff. Never assert that a position represents your final offer unless it actually does. You must retain the threat of finality for use only when you mean it. Otherwise, if your customer accepts your bluff and challenges you to live with a stand you do not want to be stuck with, your dishonesty will become apparent. He may never again accept any position you take as being your final position. This opens you to the risk of having even your ultimate fallback position overrun.

Model Scenario of Falling Back

CUSTOMER: I not only want aluminum at the price of steel; I want the easy-opening feature at no additional charge.

SALESMAN: [Buying time by introducing a distracting element.] There's no way we could give you an equal price on an order of anything less than 50 million units. [Appealing

to a third party for help.] Even then, I'd have to get a
specific O. K. from Contract & Price.

CUSTOMER: When could you know?

SALESMAN: End of the week at the latest. [Building suspense.] If we can swing it, you'll have a genuine exclusive
on the package. You really don't need the easy-opening
end to give you exclusivity. If you want it, though, I can
get you an excellent price.

CUSTOMER: Why can't I have it as part of the deal?

SALESMAN: [Taking a stand.] I don't dare ask for it. If I did,
it could endanger the aluminum price. Let's leave it the
way it is for now.

Take a Stand

You can also take a stand at any point during a defense in
depth. When you dig in, you create a standoff. A standoff tells
the customer that this is the best you can do for him. It is your
final fallback—the end of the line. In taking your stand there,
you can appeal to one or more of four restrictions:

Ethical considerations. If you appeal to ethics, don't
preach or take a superior attitude by talking down to the
customer. It is not necessary to make him feel unethical in
order to establish your own ethical restraints.

Legal considerations. Be prepared to quote a relevant
chapter and verse to document your interpretation.

Corporate policy. There is no rationale for policy. It says
what it says because that's what it says.

Custom, tradition, and precedent. Anything that has never
been done before can probably be put off at least one more
time.

You can take a stand based on time considerations as well as
on a position. An offer can have a time limit attached to it, after
which it expires. Time is an important consideration in another
context as well. When you rest your case and the customer
continues to stick to his demand without softening it, you can
create an impasse. An impasse carries with it the implication

that you have all the time in the world to wait. If you do, fine. If not, you can use the stalemated time to plan how to break the deadlock. You may reopen negotiation by coming back with a particular interpretation of policy or the law that will permit you to go ahead. Or you may have to return to negotiation with a new fallback plan.

Before you take a stand in negotiation, you should consider two potential problems. Your customer may become angry or frustrated by your stand and the delay it imposes. He may never get over it, or he may go elsewhere to buy.

Model Scenario of Taking a Stand

CUSTOMER: So that's it—the best you can do for me?

SALESMAN: [Taking his stand.] I'm afraid so. [Using the "we" approach to become partners.] We'd have two problems if we tried to improve on the deal. [Implying that the deal is already pretty good.] One is the law. We'd be skirting it. The other is policy. Why give ourselves a hard time when we have so much more room for maneuver in making available other benefits. [Implying a trade-off.]

CUSTOMER: You mean about the discount? Exactly what can you do for me there?

Trade Off

When a negotiation reaches the point where you feel you can successfully conclude its defense, you can offer to trade off something you can afford to give in return for the customer's agreement. The ideal trade-off allows the customer to perceive that he is receiving greater value than he is giving up. This is the definition of a bargain: a trade whose perceived value is greater than its price. Most customers define bargains as being deals in their favor. In no case should the customer perceive that the bargain is yours.

A tit-for-tat trade should not be so literally construed that you feel you can give up only one position in return for exactly one of the customer's demands. You may want to offer a small package of two or more positions in return for one concession.

The numbers are irrelevant. It is the perceived value of what is being bartered that matters. As long as you retain positions you cannot afford to yield and give up positions your customer perceives as important to him, a trade-off can be equitable.

Some trade-offs may contain a deferred concession plus an immediate consideration. This helps soften the blow for you. It may also help spread out the benefit for your customer. Another form of deferred concession is the option. Instead of actually yielding a hard and fast point, you can promise a future benefit whose precise nature is left open. This can result in spreading out any negative effects you may experience as the result of your barter. It may also work out so that you end up conceding nothing at all if the customer fails to exercise his option.

There are two cautions to keep in mind when you make a trade-off. One is to avoid making your offer too early in the negotiation. That might minimize its impact. It might also lead to encouraging your customer to demand even more from you since he could then believe your offer is only the first part of a step-by-step fallback and there is more to come.

A second caution is to offer neither too little nor too much. Too little an offer will lead to continued pressure for further concessions and will not result in a trade. Too great an offer may cause the customer to question the true value of what he will receive from you or your motive in offering it. It might make him suspect either your offer or your integrity, and perhaps both.

Model Scenario of a Trade-off

CUSTOMER: One of your competitors is offering a case allowance of a third more than you're offering. Another supplier, a regional, can stock us with 20 percent free goods plus a saturation TV campaign.

SALESMAN: We don't match allowances because we don't have to. But in this kind of situation where we both have so much going for us [trying to become partners], I can improve our allowance for this one time. [Preserving his options for another trade-off at a later date.]

CUSTOMER: Is that all?

SALESMAN: [Deferring a concession.] I'll request a boost in your free goods to cover the early introductory period. [Limiting the trade.] But I'll expect you to handle any remainders, O.K.? [Making the trade.]

Turnaround

Whenever you are placed on the defensive, consider one of the three forms of turnaround to help you restore a cooperative negotiation. One way is to act first when you sense a customer's complaint or request coming. By taking the initiative, you may be able to steal his thunder by defusing his argument. State his complaint or make his request before he does. But present it in the form of why the complaint has no substance or why the request, if it was actually made, could not be honored.

You may be able to take the sting out of a complaint by saying something like this: "This is the kind of situation where it would be easy for your people to blame my people for the problem and vice versa. Incidentally, my people are strongly committed to making their contribution. They're really dedicated to getting this installation going for you. Your people probably feel the same intense dedication. This is the kind of situation, as you well know, that could lead to all kinds of emotional venting unless cooler heads prevail. You and I are going to have to be those cooler heads."

If you anticipate a request instead of a complaint, you can try to head it off by casually dropping a warning like this into the conversation: "A few of our customers are trying to use the present situation of industry overcapacity to talk prices down. But our costs are simply too high to give us any leeway and we've had to tell them so." Or you can say, "We've had so many requests for trial installations that we've had to adopt a moratorium on them for the next quarter or so." At this point, you are in position to make an exception of the customer by granting him the request you expect him to make even before he makes it. You can attach a price tag to it by making it part of a trade-off or you can give it away.

The two other forms of turnaround are renovating a customer's argument or repositioning the customer himself. If you choose the renovation approach, you will have to be ready to inject into the negotiation a new set of facts that refute the customer's facts or at least his interpretation of them. By making the argument new, you can create a counterpoint in the negotiation that may turn his attention away from his prepared proof and turn his hostility or confusion into a need to understand something new. If you help him achieve this understanding, the two of you can reinforce your partnership by sharing in new learning together.

If you cannot renovate an argument, you will have to try to reposition the customer who is making the complaint. A customer who comes at you complainingly is playing the role of aggrieved aggressor. He is the attacker. He wants to win. As long as he continues to play this role, you can only play the role of loser or, at best, defender. To restore yourself to being an equal negotiator, you must try to turn the customer around to a different positioning.

The best repositioned role into which he can be transformed is that of teacher, not aggressor. This allows you to reposition yourself as his pupil, not his victim. Instead of his complaint, you can then receive his lesson. Instead of defending yourself, you can apply yourself to implementing your customer's teachings or counsel with him on how to adapt them so they can be applied. By positioning him as teacher, you render him benign. By demonstrating to him that you have learned the lesson, you may be able to turn him around to take a more cooperative approach to you and to the problem by starting up the teach-learn cycle once again.

Model Scenario of a Turnaround

CUSTOMER: Many of our people are getting restless for results on your project. Frankly, I'm jumpy myself. I'm having a hard time saying no to requests that I cancel out at the next cutoff point and get out of the whole deal.

SALESMAN: [Trying to reposition the customer into a teacher.] We're all frustrated by the unexpected pace of this one project. Please let me have the benefit of your best thinking on how we can reduce the aggravation on your side. Will you help me work out a remedial program that will hold the fort for us while we bring the project home?

Call for Help

If you are unable to gain defensive leverage by yourself, call for help from a corporate staff expert or outside authority who will lend credibility to your right to negotiate. Or you can ask for help from another customer whose testimonial in your behalf will be credited by your customer as honest and relevant.

By calling for help, you will be using a third party's foot in the door as leverage. Once he opens the door for you, it will be up to you to put your own best foot forward and keep the door open. Do not rely on a third party to maintain your position indefinitely for you. As soon as you are strong enough to negotiate on your own, abandon your crutch. This does not mean that you should abandon the authority. It simply means that you should stand on your own two feet as quickly as possible by managing the authority's contribution and acting as its interpreter and applications expert.

Since satisfied customers can often provide the most impressive third-party references, you should build a portfolio of case histories for help in negotiation. Organize them on a problem/solution basis. When you refer to a case, select one that shows the successful solution of a problem similar to the customer's current problem. Present the solution in terms of its end-result benefits, especially the benefits of improved customer profit from either reduced costs or increased sales revenues.

Case histories may not be a substitute for the personal testimony of a satisfied customer, but they can act to reassure your customer. They can also serve as a helpful sample of the kind of testimonial you may request from the customer you are negotiating with when he is asked to bear witness to your credibility.

You must be careful not to imply a partnership between you

and an expert in alliance against a customer. Your alliance must always be with your customer. The presence of a third party should be used as a catalyst to help you partner your customer. This does not mean that either of you must be antagonistic toward the third party. Instead, you must remain independent of him.

Model Scenario of Calling for Help from a Customer

CUSTOMER: I'd like to be a little bit more comfortable with your proposition before I recommend it seriously. There are several novel aspects to it that I'm sure will bother many of our people.

SALESMAN: [Calling for help.] That's why I asked Ed Jones of the XYZ Company to meet with us. A year ago he was in the same position as you are now: anxious to go ahead with us to capitalize on an unusually advantageous opportunity and needing some support. He'll take you through his own experience so you can see the parallels.

CUSTOMER: Does Jones have results yet?

SALESMAN: Jones has results. After he lays them out for us, you and I will then translate them to fit your own situation. [Becoming partners.]

Model Scenario of Calling for Help from an Expert

CUSTOMER: Have you found a way yet to make your low-cost system work for us?

SALESMAN: [Calling for help.] Dr. Smith here has had the two top men on his R&D staff trying to work out a fit. They're smart enough to do it. But they've asked me to advise you against it on the basis of cost-effectiveness.

DR. SMITH: That's right. I can show you the problems you would run into and their costs.

SALESMAN: [Reinforcing partnership with the customer.] No matter how hard we try—and you'll see how hard we really have tried—we can't win them all. But we can still achieve our original objectives with the more complete system you and I originally discussed.

Take a Walk

The defensive strategy of taking a walk has many useful applications. When your customer feels strongly about a certain point that is far more important to him than it is to you, walk away from it. Give in graciously. If you believe you can earn future leverage by giving in now, retreat slowly. Move to your eventual fallback position on a step-by-step basis so that your partner will know you are surrendering something of worth and he owes you one the next time around. At hardly any cost, you can run up a credit.

When you are wrong, cool the tendency to defend yourself anyway. Admit it. Take a called third strike and wait for your next turn at bat.

When your partner openly confronts you and you have the option of using a defensive negotiation strategy or refusing to defend, there may sometimes be a greater value in cooling it. By walking away and refusing to establish a defensive position, you can often maintain a cooperative atmosphere. Once in a while, the refusal to defend your position will so disarm your customer that he will act to restore the win-win balance in an even more cooperative manner than you yourself had planned.

In other situations such as a long and progressive fallback when you have taken your stand and made your final concession, and yet your customer persists in pressing for further considerations, your sole remaining alternative may be to walk away from the deal. By taking a walk you symbolically underline your refusal to negotiate further. You make it seem that you are going to take a long walk and get lost, maybe forever. This suggests that the next move, if there is to be one, is up to the customer.

Even though you walk away, you do not have to rule out further negotiation. After a reasonable interval, you may reinstate your willingness to bargain. But you should make it clear that you will not pick up where you left off. What was intolerable then is obviously still intolerable now. This gives you the opportunity to restore a more equal balance of forces in the negotiation so that you can take over at a stronger point. The customer must now fall back to a less aggressive position or trade off with you. If he will not concede to you, you can take another walk and try again.

It is best to limit your demands for more equitable terms in the negotiation to a change in one major issue. By focusing on only a single position, you can strengthen your claim that this point alone is preventing agreement and that the negotiation is therefore virtually assured of success if this one obstacle can be removed. This approach helps make negotiation seem more desirable than a standoff is. It also frees you from having to play the role of a long-suffering victim and allows both your customer and you to preserve your self-images as essentially reasonable negotiators.

In all these examples, forbearance acts as a negotiation strategy. Occasionally forebearance is expressed by letting something go by as swiftly as possible without reacting to it. On other occasions you will have to bide your time as a way of letting something go by slowly. And on still other occasions, when something will not go by on its own, you will have to walk away and be the one who does the going by.

Model Scenario of Taking a Walk

CUSTOMER: I hadn't planned to hear from you again on this project.

SALESMAN: [Trying to pay off a walk he had taken.] I've been trying to find a way around the problem we ran into. We still want to help you. If anyone can do it, we can.

CUSTOMER: Well, do you want to go back and review where we stand?

SALESMAN: [Retaking his stand.] Let's take a look at some of the new approaches I've been working on since our last meeting. I think you'll find they are a good deal more responsive to your problems—and have fewer drawbacks.

How to Avoid Forcing Defensiveness on Yourself

In the normal course of your customer partnerships, your partner and the challenging situations which the two of you explore together will impose enough defensive negotiation situations on you without your help. Because it is basic partnering strategy to keep defensive situations to a minimum, you should avoid forcing defensiveness on yourself. This means that you must avoid problem centering in your negotiations and concentrate on solutions to problems.

A customer partnership should be a mutual solution society. The best mutual solution arising from negotiation is mutual profit improvement. This common objective should be the focal point of all negotiation. It should be referred to frequently. It should be positioned at the outset of every negotiation as the partnership's objective. It should be restated at the conclusion of every negotiation. If a problem has required the negotiation in the first place, the problem should be discussed in the context of its solution: how mutual profit can be gained or restored.

Solutions that can deliver improved profit have the capability of uniting partners. Problems that threaten profit isolate and divide partners. While both partners want solutions, especially mutually beneficial solutions, neither partner wants a problem. Solutions have a way of being "ours." Problems tend to be "yours." If you focus your negotiations on problems, no matter what their original source may be, you risk ending up with them as yours and being identified by your customer as a problem causer—that is, a profit reducer—rather than a profit improver.

Problem centering will make you the parent of most of the partnership's problems. It can also rivet the consciousness of both of you on an endless dissection of each problem, a repetitive rehashing of its alleged causes and assumed results, and the inevitable attempts to fix blame. Even worse, problems have a way of sticking in customer memories. If you center on problem A, something about it will trigger a recollection of a similar cause or result in problem B, which in turn is reminiscent of problem C. The partnership then takes on an aura of fallibility, and you are most likely to appear to be the central problem yourself.

Whenever you use the words, "We have a problem" or whenever you introduce a negotiation by saying, "We can't get anywhere until we first solve this problem," you are practically guaranteeing a problem orientation for the negotiation. You are also opening yourself to accusation. "Well, whose problem is it, anyway?" When this happens, discord can dominate the relationship. While the partners departner each other, mutual profit improvement falls by the wayside.

A simple rule will help you avoid problem centering: no problem identification without a solution suggestion. Start talking solution from the outset. Introduce the problem in the context of the solution. Make sure that you and the customer are talking about the same problem and that you agree on the need to solve it and on its priority in the relationship. Whenever the problem is referred to, relate it immediately to its solution. Create what psychologists call "closure." Leave the negotiation the same way you began it by repeating the solution.

10
How to Anticipate and Resolve Conflict

In just about any ongoing customer relationship, some periods of contention are inevitable. Even though both you and your customer recognize that you have a sizable stake in maintaining the harmony of the relationship, your customer may get out of control or forces beyond his control may cause tensions or put unusual pressures on him. When these situations occur—as they often do in such cases as materials allocations, changes in price or delivery date or conditions, and callbacks or other quality control problems—the burden will probably fall largely or entirely on you to resolve the impending or actual conflict in a way that preserves the negotiable base of the relationship.

In this chapter we will explore the most common events causing a need to negotiate and the two basic types of strategies you can use to avoid conflict or to confront conflict successfully if it comes.

Common Pitfalls and Pratfalls to Anticipate

The three basic events requiring customer negotiation—customer requests, customer complaints, and innovations that can be introduced into your relationship by either of you—recur because they are inherent in the essential nature of selling. From a human relations point of view, they are integral parts of the sale. Because certain pitfalls and pratfalls are repetitive over time with every customer, their occurrence can confidently be predicted in the course of negotiating your way around the problems they present. If you can anticipate these negative circumstances before they happen and if you can plan your reactions to them, your negotiation strategies will take on an enhanced likelihood of success.

A few problem situations are virtually common denominators in all customer-salesman relations. Four are concerned with product: samples, modifications, callbacks and returns, and allocation. Two are concerned with certain aspects of your own performance on a day-to-day basis and when you are making proposals. Two more are concerned with price and credit or finance. The final two problem situations have to do with promotional support services and dealer or distributor relations.

Pitfalls and Pratfalls in Product Situations

Sampling

When your customer requests a sample, a product prototype, or a trial installation, don't just give it to him. Trade it off by negotiating for a commitment from him in turn. Or you can perhaps trade it off for some knowledge, especially information about competitive sampling policies. Even when you have made a win-win type of trade-off, still don't give the sample away. Quantify its dollar cost and make sure your customer perceives the value he is receiving. Also make sure you know the identity of the decision maker or influencer who is requesting the sample so you can include him in your continuing coverage of the account.

Modifications

In handling customer requests for product modifications, watch particularly for two pitfalls. One is to negotiate by acquiescing too readily to the request and failing to determine the need for modification (or for the particular modification requested), or failing to correlate the projected benefits from the modification with what you know about your customer's market needs. The other pitfall is to create a conflict situation by taking a negative stand at the outset and rejecting consideration of a product change.

Before you adopt a point of view, talk to your customer's engineers, manufacturing people, sales managers, product managers, and anyone else in his company who may be involved. Find out what they think before you let them know what you think. Then, if you decide to negotiate, consult with your company's technical people before you commit to modification.

Callbacks and Returns

To convert a product-return request into a negotiable situation that offers you the opportunity to win something, make a hard resell effort at a trade-off. Research in depth the reasons your customer gives for requesting to return the product. Don't contest them until you have probed their validity. If they are incontestable, learn from them and pass your learning along to your sales and technical people. If your customer has been forced to call back any of his own products because of a failure of your own product, improve your negotiating position by adding an offer to help find a new home for his returns.

Allocation

Rule one of allocation negotiations is early warning. If you notify a customer at a time that he perceives as too late to fit in with his own planning cycle, you will immediately be put in a defensive and perhaps even indefensible position. When you must present an allocation notice, be prepared with facts that explain why it is necessary, what its terms are, and how long its probable duration may be. By demonstrating empathy for the customer's problems, you solidify the basis for partnership with him in working through the situation. Be helpful. Suggest substitute materials or alternative suppliers. You may have to allocate your product but you don't have to hold back on consultative aid and comfort.

Pitfalls and Pratfalls in Performance Situations

Handling Accounts

If you discover a deficiency in how you handle a customer's business, do two things. First, remedy it. Second, communicate your discovery and its remedy to your customer. Don't announce your discovery without having a remedy ready or, even better, have it already in use.

If you attempt to cover up your deficiency and it surfaces, you will be hard-pressed to negotiate a defense. Stonewalling as a defense is not a negotiation strategy that will make you and your customer partners. The best defense in handling errors of omission or commission in an account, of course, is to make changes before the problems occur. This is a leadership strategy. It allows you to quantify the dollar value of your innovation in terms of return on investment. It also allows you to stress the custom-tailored nature of your service and so helps you brand it distinctively and distinguish it from the competition.

Rejecting Proposals

When a customer rejects a proposal, he is actually making a request of you: Understand my needs better and react to them more fittingly. He is, in effect, inviting you to be innovative and come back to him with a new approach. If you adopt this attitude, you will use rejection as a basis for negotiation and not as an excuse to withdraw or to persuade the customer to accept your proposal anyway. Instead of attempting to resell the original proposal, trade off his rejection for an opportunity to improve your knowledge of his needs. React immediately. This can give you the opportunity to gain access to decision makers and influencers you would not otherwise be able to contact. Your revised proposal can then contain your customer's thinking as well as your own in a jointly developed and jointly beneficial recommendation for mutually improved profits.

Pitfalls and Pratfalls in Money Situations

Pricing

Every time you tamper with price you alter the customer's perception of value. Price negotiations are tests of your belief in the combined value of your products and services, your personal expertise in applying them to improve your customer's profit, and the information base you have at your disposal to help you make successful applications. If you yield by accepting a lower price without trading off some value, you will destroy the high value-to-price relationship you must maintain in order to command a premium price. Where you have no unique value to trade for price, you will put yourself in a commodity position that allows the customer to determine price. This means that you should always be able to justify price maintenance by proving added value. And when you must cut back in price, cut out some of the value that it represents.

Credit and Finance

A customer who requests credit is negotiating a form of price concession with you. This means that your value-to-price relationship is once again going to be challenged. Protect it by making your recommendation for a credit extension represent an added value of doing business with you. If you cannot trade off on the added value at the moment, stockpile it for future use. Keep your customer informed of your role as his agent in your internal negotiations with credit and collection people. Position yourself as your customer's partner in his perception of you. Use your ability to provide credit as a justification for maintaining your premium price and favored supplier status.

Pitfalls and Pratfalls in Dealer and Distributor Situations

When a customer moves important volume through dealers or distributors, you should consider these people as a second but different level of customer. Remember that they are independent businessmen, probably much more entrepreneurial than your customer. This means that profit is necessarily the name of their game. Be sure you understand how your customer's products affect their profit and how you can help them increase it. Learn how their needs differ from your customer's needs. Help them solve their unique problems and capitalize on their opportunities. You can often improve your own profitable sales volume considerably by helping a customer's dealers and distributors move more of your customer's products. You can accomplish this objective best if you negotiate with them as businessmen who have their own needs rather than simply as local sales outlets.

Pitfalls and Pratfalls in Promotional Support Situations

Requests for promotional support are also a way of asking for price concessions. Therefore the same negotiation pitfall encountered in the maintenance of your value-to-price relationship applies equally to promotion requests as to credit. If you provide free or cooperative customer support, trade it off for a value in return, especially in the form of information. Put a value on the support services you provide, and thereby stockpile future trade-offs. If you cannot recommend free support for a customer, don't reject his request; form a partnership with him to create no-cost or low-cost support programs for him to execute, such as tie-in sales, special events, seasonal promotions, and cooperative ventures with third parties.

How to Avoid Conflict

You can choose from six strategies to avoid confronting a customer who appears about to come in conflict with you:

1. Turn the other cheek
2. Buy time
3. Yield diagonally
4. Wave a red flag

5. Hire an agent
6. Refer to arbitration

Turn the Other Cheek

Conflict will often pass right by you if you turn away from it. At worst it will glance off you without harm. If you plan to turn aside, you will have to be prepared to hang in there when your customer confronts you, moving only your cheek. If you move more than that, you run the risk that your customer will perceive you as squirming or—even worse—fleeing.

By turning aside, you allow the customer to get off his chest whatever it is that bothers him. You permit him to confront you without being confronted by you in turn. This means you will have to hold your tongue and your temper in the interests of keeping the situation from becoming worse.

When you turn your cheek away from the onslaught of the customer's argument, you must adopt the role of interested and sympathetic listener. This doesn't mean you must agree with everything your customer says. But you must pay attention, take him seriously, refrain from disputing his points of view, and encourage him to go on until he has thoroughly ventilated his views. From time to time during his recitation, probe him by requesting amplification, either in the form of factual documentation or further opinion. You can underline your serious interest by taking notes. By concentrating on note taking, you can avoid eye contact that might encourage further confrontation with your customer. Keeping yourself busy will also help you stay cool.

At the conclusion of the customer's argument, you have a choice of three options if you're still determined to avoid conflict. You can buy time by promising to study the matter. This may enable you to come back with factual support. Or you can yield diagonally to his arguments. Or finally you can suggest an arbitrator or mediator.

Model Scenario of Turning the Other Cheek

CUSTOMER: I'm very unhappy about the way the whole problem has been handled. We've dropped other suppliers from our approval list for giving us a good deal less trouble. Do you have any idea how many of our operations have been affected by your performance—or lack of it?

SALESMAN: [Turning the other cheek.] Based on your question, I have the feeling that they may be even more widespread than I know. Will you quickly enumerate them for me?

CUSTOMER: Just put down the whole plant. And while you're at it, put down what you're going to do to get us out of this mess.

SALESMAN: That's exactly what I want to do on a problem-by-problem basis. So I hope you'll take a few minutes to review how each of your operations has been affected. [Asking the customer to amplify so he can ventilate fully.] Then [buying time] I'm going to set up an emergency meeting with our people tonight [showing interest and sympathy] so I can come right back to you in 48 hours with a solution-by-solution approach.

Buy Time

Some antagonistic situations are too hot to handle. You need to let them simmer down before you can touch them. If a customer's attitude is so bad that it can't get worse, time is on your side. Buy time. Put off saying or doing anything except promising to do something right away.

There are three immediate actions you can take to get the ball rolling and convince your customer that you are taking him seriously. All three have one characteristic in common: they give time a chance to act as the great healer and so hold off conflict.

The first thing you can do is to promise to study the matter immediately and report back on your findings by a specific date. The date must be soon. Make an appointment right then and there for your second meeting. If the problem is technical or scientific in nature, you may want to convene a committee to make the study. If you need to demonstrate your sincerity in a dramatic way, offer to include one of the customer's associates on the committee.

Instead of holding a time-buying meeting, or as a result of it, you can offer to construct a pilot operation, a prototype installation, or an experimental application to test out a way of avoiding similar problems in the future. This prevents you from having to eat crow by apologizing or accepting blame where such self-deprecation is unwarranted. It also shows your goodwill to the customer. He can see his purposes being served by your attempt to safeguard your mutual interests for the future. He can also channel his energies away from complaining onto a more creative undertaking: making a new approach work in partnership with you.

The third option is to focus on a planned way of working together to avoid further problems or to seize new opportunities. Offer to put together an outline of a plan to harmonize your participation in the next project, thus implying there will be a next project, and then put the finishing touches to it with the customer. As in the case of making a study, set a date for your follow-up meeting to validate your sensitivity to the customer's urgent need. The date must be soon. While you are putting the plan together, you will be buying time in a constructive manner.

Model Scenario of Buying Time

CUSTOMER: From a personal point of view I hate to have to tell you this. But professionally our requirements have now grown to the point where we need a second supplier.

SALESMAN: I think this is an excellent time—the first time, really, that it might make sense to explore this issue—to survey the assets and liabilities of two suppliers on your account. [Buying time.] We can help you. After all, we use the second-supplier approach ourselves when we're on the outside of a piece of business looking in. I'm going to work with our technical and financial people over the next ten days and have them give you a preview of the economies and expenses you could expect if you went that way. Let's take a look at your calendar and compare available dates two weeks from now. When we meet at that time, we'll review our plan to improve the cost-effectiveness of our work together over the next six months.

Yield Diagonally

As you know, the customer is always right. The inevitable extension of the equation is that when you are wrong, you are wrong. Admit it by yielding diagonally to the customer's accusations so that you can avoid coming into conflict with him.

You can yield diagonally by using either or both of two strategies. The first avoidance strategy is "Yes, but." When you say "Yes" you are agreeing with your customer by acknowledging that he is correct. When you follow it with "but," you are yielding diagonally. On the one hand you offer agreement. On the other hand your "but" gives you the opportunity to state your own case under congenial circumstances and trade off a defensive argument against the customer's attack.

In circumstances where you may not have a "but" to your name, you will have to rest your case with a plain, unadorned "Yes." The simple honesty of agreement can be disarming, especially if it comes after several "Yes, but" trade-offs.

A second avoidance strategy is "Yes, and." This strategy preserves the "Yes, but" advantage of agreeableness under pressure and prevents even the semblance of disagreement from entering the discussion. The word "and" is reassuring. It suggests amplification of the customer's point of view, not a challenge to it. It can give you the opportunity to supplement his arguments with your own set of facts, allowing you to patch your facts onto his without creating antagonism.

If you use the "Yes, and" strategy well, your customer will often be compelled to defend himself by adopting a "Yes, but" rejoinder: "Yes, I hear what you say, but I disagree with it." Or, "Yes, but what does that have to do with our discussion?" Any time you can convert an offensive confrontation to a defensive interrogation or protestation, you are avoiding conflict and restoring a negotiable situation.

Model Scenario of Yielding Diagonally

CUSTOMER: You're just going to have to go back to the drawing board with your proposal. There's no way I can sell this to our people.

SALESMAN: There are a number of areas I've made notes on
for us to revise. I'll get them in the works at once. But
there are some parts of the proposal that are tailor-made to
your needs and I'd hate to see you lose out on them if we
were to make a general revision. Don't you agree?

CUSTOMER: Well, I didn't feel there was too much worth
saving, frankly. There's not much there we haven't seen
before.

SALESMAN: Yes, that's true. [Yielding diagonally.] And the
advantage of those elements is that they balance the areas
of the proposal that are truly unique—the ones we're going
to engineer differently, as you suggested. What we'll come
back with will be a balanced proposal that will work and
that you can sell.

CUSTOMER: Well, all right. But the burden of proof will be on
you. [Converting the customer to a ''Yes, but'' response.]

Wave a Red Flag

On occasion, and perhaps more often than you may be
aware, you can be the target of a customer's contentiousness
that you do not cause. As a salesman, you are a relatively safe
target for a customer who wants to blow off steam. Yet the
opposite is not true. It can be extremely dangerous for you to
respond in a contentious manner with a customer.

When a customer comes at you like an angry bull, you may
be able to avoid conflict with him by waving a red flag and
leading him onto another subject. This is a twofold strategy of
attraction followed by distraction.

Red-flagging will work only if the customer is angry at someone other than you. If you suspect this to be the case, try to
distract him by raising another issue. Make it an issue that
promises to benefit him if the two of you can solve it together.
This means it should have new business potential for you.
Since it is difficult to invent profitable business proposals on the
spur of the moment—especially if you are under fire—always
keep two or three propositions simmering on a back burner of
your mind. You can get at them easily in this way when you
need them.

While you're waiting out the opening blast of a customer's wrath before you attempt to distract him, patience is a virtue. If you make your move too soon, his feelings will be only partially vented. He may use his remaining frustration or anxiety to knock down your proposal regardless of its merit. So let him ventilate himself but not to a point of exhaustion or disinterest that will prevent your taking some sort of action to make things right again.

If you make the wrong assumption about the true target of a customer's hostility and it turns out to be you and you alone, your customer will let you know it in no uncertain terms. He may simply refuse to be distracted. Your effort to turn him away will add to his unhappiness with you. Applying your best judgment is therefore a prerequisite before you wave a red flag.

Model Scenario of Waving a Red Flag

CUSTOMER: I think our conclusion after the pilot test is over will be that your installation is just too costly for us at this time. We'll probably ask you to take it home again.

SALESMAN: That will leave you with the same problem you've had all along and no solution in sight.

CUSTOMER: But we won't have the added cost.

SALESMAN: Let's look at it this way for a moment. The problem isn't with the economics of the installation. [Waving the flag.] Your cost factor is inflated by the lack of experience your people have in operating the unit. That's why you've had slow production and downtime. I'd like to implement a training program with your operating people, beginning next Monday. If you'll help get them set up for it, I'm sure we can not only bring the cost down but step up output as well.

Hire an Agent

Sometimes the only way to avoid a conflict with a customer is to avoid the customer. This can be done by hiring an agent to represent you in a conflict resolution situation. As a third party, the agent can take a far less personal position in the conflict, stand reasonably above its most embarrassing or accusatory aspects, and still allow your customer to express himself and make his points.

An agent is a stand-in. He can be your boss or a peer but no one below you in rank. You cannot send a boy to do a man's job. In deputizing the agent to stand in your stead, you must give him the power of attorney to make commitments for you if he feels they are required. If an agent is skillful, the only commitment he may have to make to your customer is the promise to report fully to you on the customer's position and to recommend certain actions on your part. In this way he can buy time for you by acting as a news reporter and adviser who will speak *to* you but not *for* you.

To help ensure that your agent can turn away a customer's wrath without committing you to an unfavorable compromise or accommodation, it is best to grant him only limited power. He can thereby enter into negotiations by immediately stating his inability to commit you to any particular arrangement. This approach can subtly influence your customer to offer the agent a better deal than he might make available to you. By stressing that he can only report and recommend to you but cannot commit for you, the agent puts implicit pressure on the customer to make his best offer or his most acceptable demands. Since he can elicit no committed playback from your agent, the customer is put in the position of essentially competing with himself.

The more impressive your agent is in terms of reputation, prestige, or status, the better. Your customer must not perceive him as a substitute for you. Instead, the customer should see him as an even more desirable negotiator than you. If your agent's rank is truly high, the customer may adopt a defensive, apologetic, or even adulatory stance that will take much of the wind out of his sails. By appointing a worthy representative and positioning him as a man far more able to help solve the customer's problem, you can take the curse off any appearance of running away.

Refer to Arbitration

An arbitrator is a joint agent, representing both you and your customer when you are unable to agree. But the arbitrator differs from an agent in one major respect: He has the power to make a decision that you and your customer must previously agree to abide by. Referring a contested situation to arbitration can help depolarize it by concentrating the decision-making authority in a third party and obviating participation in a conflict yourself.

You and your customer must agree on who the arbitrator will be. He or she can be anyone you both trust to be impartial. Agreeing on the arbitrator can be your first step back toward re-creating a negotiable environment. If the arbitrator decides to settle the matter by compromise, you and your customer may acquire a second common bond in your mutual unhappiness with the arbitrator.

How to Confront Conflict

When you become skillful at resolving business conflicts by avoiding them, you will be fortunate if you can dispose of more than eight out of ten conflicting situations in this way. The other two will probably be unavoidable. You don't even have to be the direct cause of them. Just being in the wrong place at a crucial time may cause a conflict to polarize around you. On the other hand, grievances often build up spontaneously in even the best relationships. Unforeseeable events can bring unavoidable discord that threatens to invade your personal or professional "essentials." In such cases, you have three strategies to choose from to confront a conflict: look at the record, take a stand, or intimidate.

Look at the Record

The least antagonistic confrontation strategy to use in a conflict situation with your customer is to refer to the record to establish a fact base for your negotiation. This is especially important if the customer's attitude seems largely emotional.

By going to some sort of recorded facts as the basis for discussion and showing that his arguments are not supportable from an objective point of view, you can frequently take some of the heat out of a customer's demand or complaint.

When you use this approach, make it an invitation to share jointly with your customer in examining the facts. This can help re-create your partnership as a mutual undertaking. It also prevents the facts from being regarded by the customer as "your facts," which automatically opens them up to dispute. The facts should be "our facts," a shared resource.

Your ability to use a fact base as a platform for confronting conflict depends on two conditions. One is that you must have access to the fact base. You must know where to put your hands on it and how to interpret it. Facts are every salesman's most important selling tool. They can also be one of your most important negotiating aids.

The second condition is that you should be reasonably certain in advance that the facts will support your case. Otherwise they will deprive you of suggesting recourse to the record as a strategy. This puts pressure on you to be familiar with your supportive data before you try to use them, which means you should be continually doing homework to amass an information base and learn its inputs so you can refer to them with confidence.

If you do this as a matter of course, you will find that two changes can occur that will lessen the number and severity of customer confrontations. Just being able to refer to the record and to quote a summary of the facts it contains will often make consulting it unnecessary. This will restore a negotiable situation. Second, once you have established a reputation as a man who has the facts, you may not ever be confronted with a demand to see them. Having the record at your disposal is the best guarantee that you will not have to use it.

Model Scenario of Looking at the Record

CUSTOMER: There just isn't anything you have in your entire line that has the profit potential of our house brands.

I'm not going to trade off a high profit maker for a low one.

SALESMAN: That's just the point. You already are.

CUSTOMER: What do you mean? I told you I'm not.

SALESMAN: Just look at these facts with me. [Looking at the record.] Here, this is your house brand. Its profit percentage is among the highest in the store.

CUSTOMER: Like I told you. [Agreeing with the salesman on the validity of his fact base.]

SALESMAN: All right, now look over here at actual profit dollars, not percent of profit. The house brands are among the lowest in the store. Why? Because their turnover is so low. With our line, your percent of profit per item is lower, sure. But our turnover is three to six times greater so your bottom-line profit dollars are so much greater. And it's dollars you take to the bank, not percentages.

Take a Stand

A second strategy for trying to resolve conflict by confronting it is to curl your toes, dig in your heels, get your back up, and take a stand. This is the classic confrontation stance. If your customer is acting like an irresistible force, you can position yourself as an immovable object. Either he veers off or you clash. Your bet when you take a stand is that he will turn away.

Sometimes you will want to take a stand after experimenting with a series of trade-offs. On other occasions, a customer may come at you hard and fast. By doing so, he may deprive you of the option to trade off by penetrating your defenses with such a critical issue that you will find it difficult to roll back the argument to where you can bargain. You will have to give way or stand firm.

Every once in a while you will find a customer who likes to use intimidation as a negotiating strategy against you. This will require that you take stands whenever your personal or professional boundaries are infringed upon.

It is always in your best interest to confront conflict in a negotiable manner. Even if you win the confrontation by taking a firm stand, your customer will not be able to win unless you restore a negotiable relationship. For this overriding reason it is generally better not to win a conflict even if you have the goods. There is no harm in letting the customer know you are able to win; but there is a great deal of good in resisting the temptation to take advantage of your position, once you have let the customer perceive it, and then using your strength to help him win along with you. When you take a stand in this manner, you are allowing your customer to walk right up to you, examine your power, respect it, and then respect you as a person because of the way you use your power for mutual reward.

Model Scenario of Taking a Stand

CUSTOMER: If you can't sweeten the deal for us, I can't approve it.

SALESMAN: We'll do everything we can to make it work for you. I'll even put more of my own personal time into it to give it everything it requires.

CUSTOMER: [Turning down the salesman's attempted trade-off.] What it requires is sweetening if it's going to have a chance to work here.

SALESMAN: [Trying one more trade-off.] I'll have my top customer service manager in residence here during start-up week, how's that?

CUSTOMER: That's not going to do it.

SALESMAN: Let's go over it one more time to see if we can get it to work, because that's really the maximum I can commit myself to. [Taking a stand.]

Intimidate

Intimidation is threatening to take recourse to an undesirable action. It is the ultimate strategy you can use to confront conflict with a customer in a negotiable manner. Your objective is to avoid taking recourse to the action you threaten to take. But you must not bluff. You must be prepared to go all the way and carry out your threat unless a negotiable situation can be restored. If you bluff and your customer calls your bluff, you may forfeit the relationship. You may also forfeit the relationship if you carry out your threat. This is why intimidation should be your final alternative.

You can probably use intimidation only once in any customer relationship. If it works, your relationship will be strengthened by your having shared the common experience with your customer of having walked together to the brink, having looked over the edge, and having survived. This is showdown strategy. If it doesn't work, one or both of you may go for a fall.

You can threaten recourse to four major actions if you want to intimidate a customer. The least dangerous is a threat to withdraw from your relationship by requesting a transfer or bringing in another salesman on the account.

A second action you have recourse to is a threat to take the problem upstairs to the top of the customer's organization, or at least as close to the top as you may have to go to reach the level of authority you require. A third possible action is a threat to make the problem public by means of other people who will inevitably learn of the conflict and use their knowledge for their own selfish purposes, in spite of your best efforts to ensure privacy. The fourth and final action you have recourse to is a threat to go to the law.

Just as the mutual give and take of negotiation is a win-win relationship, mutual intimidation is a two-edged sword that can create a lose-lose relationship. At best, stalemate may result. Neither of you may profit. At worst, a productive situation can go down the drain. Yet if you use intimidation sparingly and well and only in the most difficult situations you face, it can give you a confrontation tool that has the power to make the relationship equitable and therefore negotiable again.

Model Scenario of Intimidating

CUSTOMER: There's no possible benefit I can see in going over the whole deal again. If it didn't work the first time, it won't work the second time.

SALESMAN: I guess that takes us out of the running then. I'm

going to have to withdraw my company from the bidding.
CUSTOMER: When we invite a supplier to bid, we expect a bid
we can consider. If we don't get one from you, what
you've really done is squeeze out another supplier who
could have put through a deal we could consider.
SALESMAN: We think we're a logical source for you to consider. Perhaps we ought to get a third opinion to reinforce
yours and mine. [Intimidating.] Why not come upstairs
with me and see if some of your management people can
look at our proposal in a way that will help you and me see
it in a new light?

How to Practice Your Anticipation Skills

Anticipators are made, not born. You can make yourself a
better negotiator by practicing your skill in anticipating pitfalls
and pratfalls in common negotiation situations. There are three
methods that can provide you with realistic practice on a day-
to-day basis. One method is to *collect negotiated situations*
that you can use as case histories in your dealings with customers. A second method is to *rehearse negotiated solutions* to
problems that you come across in your business or personal life
even though you may not be directly involved in them. The
third method is to *serve as a consultant* to your fellow salesmen on their own negotiation problems so that you can add to
the range and depth of your anticipation capabilities.

Collect Negotiated Situations

If you keep your ears open, you can hear all around you the
evidence of other people's negotiations. When people tell you
their "troubles," they are often actually recounting a cooperative or defensive negotiation they have been engaged in and are
telling you how they have handled it. In listening to them, you
may be able to hear how they have traded off, turned a situation around, defended themselves in depth, or finally had to
take a stand. In their "He said—then I said" or "He did—so I
did," they will be telling you how they have resolved conflict
by turning the other cheek, buying time, or hiring an agent to
negotiate for them.

We suggest that you collect these vignettes that people tell you directly or that you overhear. Extract the lessons they can teach you and incorporate them into your knowledge base. Some will be humorous enough for you to inject into your customer negotiations as icebreakers. You can use others to document a point or prove the universal nature of a human response.

Rehearse Negotiated Solutions

Good negotiators are always negotiating. That may be why they are good negotiators. They use negotiation strategies in just about every interpersonal situation they encounter, whether they need to or not. This keeps them in practice. It also prevents bad negotiation habits from creeping into their style.

You will find that many experienced negotiators play imaginary negotiation games whenever they have conceptual downtime. As they walk, drive a car, or fly in an airplane, or as they enjoy leisure activity or exercise, they will simulate negotiation situations and act out both roles. Some negotiators make the situations they rehearse as realistic as possible. Others like to fabricate the toughest possible situations, combining the people and characteristics of several actual situations into one. In these fantasy negotiations, they rehearse on an as-if basis—as if the situations were real and they must be prepared to deal with them.

We suggest that you make your mind a theatrical stage and conduct at least a couple of rehearsed negotiations on it every day in the most realistic possible manner. Project yourself into both your own and your customer's role so that you can reproduce the intellectual and emotional reactions of each negotiator. Use actual dialog. Picture the negotiation in your mind so that you can see the body language, the gestures, and the facial expressions and can hear the tones of voice with your inner eyes and ears. Explore several optional endings to each negotiation. Be careful not to make them too easy on yourself or too unrealistically hard on your customers.

Consult

Your fellow salesman, either voluntarily or unwittingly, are all collectors of negotiated situations. If you consult with them about the problems they are encountering, the strategies they use, and how they are working out, you can probably vastly increase your opportunities to anticipate pitfalls and pratfalls by experiencing them on a vicarious basis.

We suggest that you offer yourself as a sounding board for other salesmen. When appropriate, give them counsel as a test of your own knowledge. Pay careful attention to the nature of each negotiation situation, the strategies being employed, and their outcomes. If you can establish yourself as a worthwhile consultant, other salesmen will bring you their experiences on a continuing basis, replenishing your opportunities to learn new sales negotiation strategies and providing you with new insights into yourself and into the common bonds you share with your partners in profit making—your customers.

Index